MW01133690

Financial Literacy
Lessons & Activities

Grade
1

All illustrations and photography, including those from Shutterstock.com, are protected by copyright.

Writing: Rachel D'Orsaneo
Content Editing: Kathleen Jorgensen
Lisa Vitarisi Mathews
Copy Editing: Laurie Westrich
Art Direction: Yuki Meyer
Cover Design: Yuki Meyer
Illustration: Mary Rojas
Design/Production: Paula Acojido
Yuki Meyer

EMC 3121

Evan-Moor®

Visit
teaching-standards.com
to view a correlation
of this book.
This is a free service.

**Correlated to
Current Standards**

**Congratulations on your purchase of some of the
finest teaching materials in the world.**

*Photocopying the pages in this book
is permitted for single-classroom use only.
Making photocopies for additional classes
or schools is prohibited.*

For information about other Evan-Moor products, call 1-800-777-4362,
fax 1-800-777-4332, or visit our website, www.evan-moor.com.
Entire contents © 2022 Evan-Moor Corporation
18 Lower Ragsdale Drive, Monterey, CA 93940-5746. Printed in USA.

CPSIA: McNaughton & Gunn, Saline, MI USA [10/2022]

Why Teach Financial Literacy?

Preparing students to understand financial concepts in school and in the real world includes teaching them about money and giving them the information that they need to be informed consumers. The foundational concepts of earning, buying, saving, and borrowing can be taught at the earliest grade levels, when children start developing habits with money. The concepts of investing and protecting money can be introduced a few years later.

For many people, transactions frequently happen electronically through tap-and-go technology in stores, online shopping, and electronic funds transfers to pay bills. Some children may rarely see actual money changing hands. This may mean that they have less opportunity to connect money's value to the things it buys. Handling bills and coins, even if they are play money, gives children a concrete understanding of how we use money to get other things of value.

Having information about how the financial world works helps people make appropriate decisions for themselves to meet their own needs and goals. Young adults need to be prepared before stepping fully into an adult's world, where there are so many risks for making mistakes with money. While people's choices are personal and may vary widely from one person to the next, everyone must find a way to navigate through a variety of financial structures.

As you present financial concepts to students, consider their diverse backgrounds and their varying world views, encouraging them to form their own opinions and share their ideas about spending, saving, credit, and more. As students grow and change, their approach to financial literacy concepts and skills may also change. It is important to provide them the tools they need so they can make the best decisions for themselves and to empower them with a solid foundation to become informed consumers who have their own financial identities.

Contents

Student Resource/Reference Pages

Units

Financial Concepts: The value of a good or service is what you would trade for it.
Money acts as a standard measure of value to make trading easy.
Trading (buying and selling) involves cooperative exchanges.

> **Math Skills:** skip counting, addition, currency

Financial Concepts: While we need foods and some items to live, other foods and items are wants.
Shoppers need to prioritize what is most important, especially if money is limited.

> **Math Skills:** addition, subtraction, currency

Financial Concepts: Decisions made about clothing involve many features that need to be ranked.
Clothing purchases need to fit the purpose and the wearer.

> **Math Skills:** addition, subtraction, currency

Financial Concepts: Money from gifts or chores provides valuable experience in spending.
Spending money develops a sense of items' worth and value.
Money earned for chores helps connect responsibility and effort to earning.

> **Math Skills:** skip counting, addition, subtraction, currency

Financial Literacy Lessons and Activities • EMC 3121 • © Evan-Moor Corporation

What's in *Financial Literacy Lessons and Activities*

Financial Literacy Lessons and Activities lets students get hands-on with personal finance. Based on national standards from the Council for Economic Education and the Jump$tart Coalition, these lessons and activities make using money concrete for students in real-life situations.

10 Engaging Units

Financial Literacy Lessons and Activities offers 10 units on grade-level topics involving the use of money. Each unit's topic focuses on a place where money is spent, things that money is spent on, or ways to receive money. The units bring together vocabulary and financial concepts using a story and explicit instruction. Practice includes math application problems and an engaging activity.

Unit Features

Units are designed to fit into a weekly lesson plan. Each 12-page unit provides information for the teacher, a story, vocabulary, concept practice, math application, and an activity.

Teacher Overview

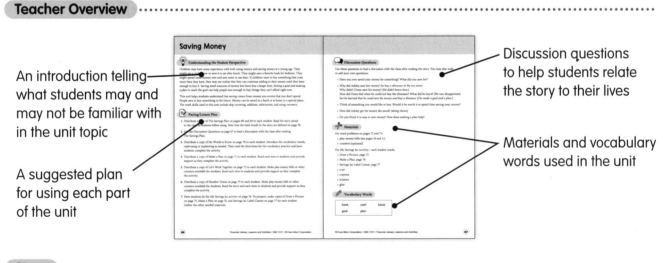

An introduction telling what students may and may not be familiar with in the unit topic

A suggested plan for using each part of the unit

Discussion questions to help students relate the story to their lives

Materials and vocabulary words used in the unit

Story

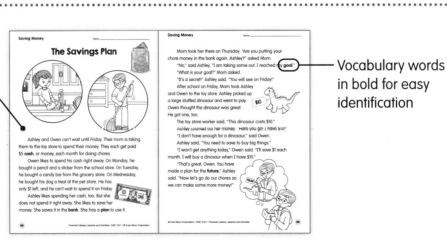

A two-page story that introduces the topic in context, as well as the vocabulary that students will learn

Vocabulary words in bold for easy identification

Vocabulary and Concept Practice

Definitions and practice writing the words in context sentences

An open-ended way to practice the concept

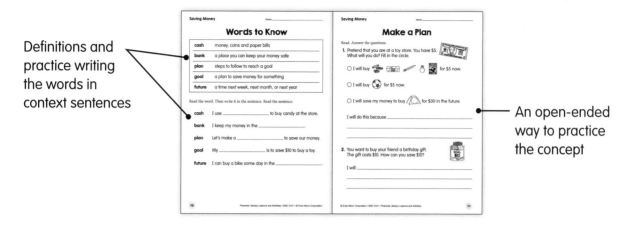

Math Application

Scenarios using money-based word problems; manipulatives and other aids provided

Scaffolding provided for multistep problems

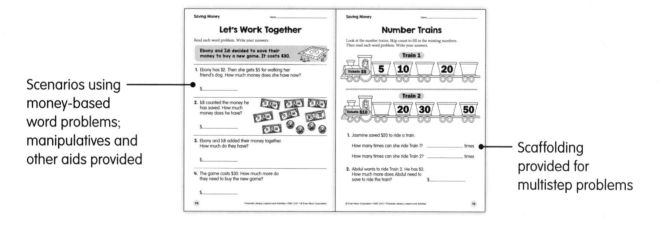

Activity

A fun art activity, game, role-play, or other activity that lets students practice using money in the unit's context

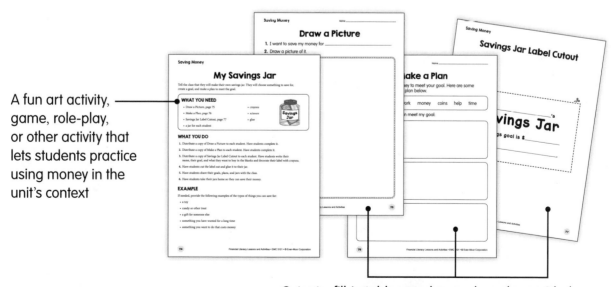

Cutouts, fill-in tables, and game boards provided

Cutouts, reference sheets, and other aids support student learning through all units:

Play money dollar bills to use as manipulatives and in games

Play money coins and higher bills to use as manipulatives

Coin equations to reinforce the value representations of coins

Add to 20 table to help with math facts

Money place-value mat for sorting coins, adding, and subtracting

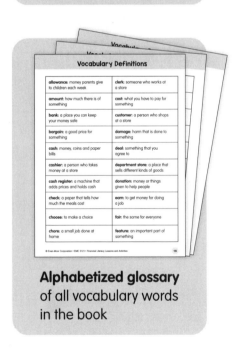

Alphabetized glossary of all vocabulary words in the book

Answer Key

Provided for the Math Application pages. The correct answer or a sample response is shown unless the question is completely open-ended.

How to Use *Financial Literacy Lessons and Activities*

Support for Consumers-to-Be

Encourage students to relate the concepts and experiences they read about to their own lives. Be mindful not to judge their choices or habits and to respect cultural and family attitudes toward using money. Tell them how money works, not how they should or shouldn't use it.

Key Words

As you decide which, if not all, of the pages in each unit you will print out for your students, be sure to include the Words to Know page that defines key concept terms. This page is useful throughout the unit. Have students tape it to their desks for easy reference. If you send a page home for homework, send the Words to Know page, as well, for support.

The Importance of Discussion

There is no one right way to earn, spend, or save money. Facilitate student discussions so that they can share ideas, thoughts, and habits. Learning from others' successes and struggles improves planning and problem-solving skills.

Connections to Other Subjects

The units in this book provide opportunities to describe characters, identify sequence and cause and effect, and increase vocabulary (reading/language arts). The units augment learning about different people's needs and wants, how a community works together, and taking responsibility (social studies). The word problems let students practice handling money, basic arithmetic, and reasoning (math).

Keeping It Playful

Use play money frequently. Consider having a good supply of play money ready before starting to use the book and collecting it after each lesson to use throughout the year. The activities at the ends of the units provide opportunities for students to work together, use hands-on materials, make decisions for themselves, and often create something meaningful.

For Non-U.S. Classrooms

While this book uses U.S. coins and bills, it can be used in any country. If your country's main denomination is not the dollar, substitute *euro, yuan, pound, rupee, riyal,* or whatever is appropriate along with your equivalent of *cent.* Practicing one-to-many correspondence is still useful for students, as are the decision-making and reasoning challenges provided.

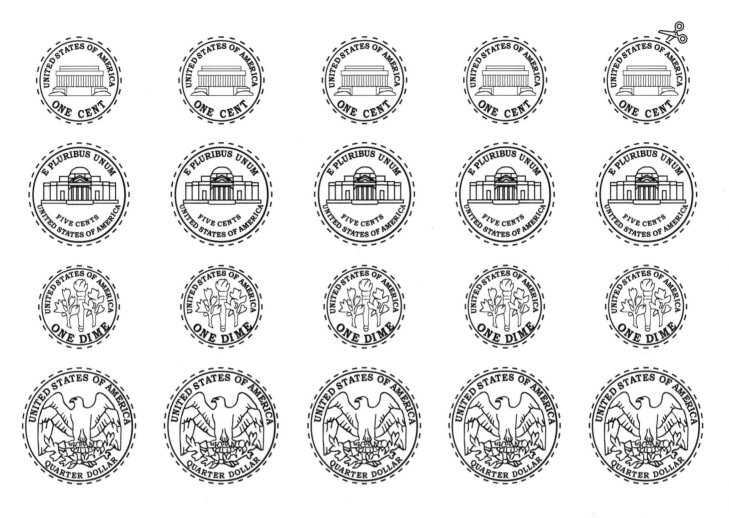

Coin Equations

1 nickel = 5 pennies

---

1 dime = 2 nickels

---

1 dime = 1 nickel and 5 pennies

---

1 quarter = 2 dimes and 1 nickel

---

1 dollar = 4 quarters

Financial Literacy Lessons and Activities • EMC 3121 • © Evan-Moor Corporation

Add to 20 Table

+	1	2	3	4	5	6	7	8	9	10
1	2	3	4	5	6	7	8	9	10	11
2	3	4	5	6	7	8	9	10	11	12
3	4	5	6	7	8	9	10	11	12	13
4	5	6	7	8	9	10	11	12	13	14
5	6	7	8	9	10	11	12	13	14	15
6	7	8	9	10	11	12	13	14	15	16
7	8	9	10	11	12	13	14	15	16	17
8	9	10	11	12	13	14	15	16	17	18
9	10	11	12	13	14	15	16	17	18	19
10	11	12	13	14	15	16	17	18	19	20

Money Place-Value Mat

Dollars (100s)	Dimes (10s)	Pennies (1s)

Vocabulary Definitions

allowance: money parents give to children each week	**clerk:** someone who works at a store
amount: how much there is of something	**cost:** what you have to pay for something
bank: a place you can keep your money safe	**customer:** a person who shops at a store
bargain: a good price for something	**damage:** harm that is done to something
cash: money, coins and paper bills	**deal:** something that you agree to
cashier: a person who takes money at a store	**department store:** a place that sells different kinds of goods
cash register: a machine that adds prices and holds cash	**donation:** money or things given to help people
check: a paper that tells how much the meals cost	**earn:** to get money for doing a job
choose: to make a choice	**fair:** the same for everyone
chore: a small job done at home	**feature:** an important part of something

flood: a lot of water inside a home	**order:** to ask for something you want to eat
for sale: can be bought	**package:** an item sent in a box
fundraiser: a way to gather money for something	**plan:** steps to follow to reach a goal; to decide what to do
future: a time next week, next month, or next year	**price:** how much something costs
gift: something given to someone	**product:** something you buy at a store
goal: a plan to save money for something	**secondhand:** something that is used
mailbox: a box used to hold mail	**server:** a person who helps people at a restaurant
menu: a list of choices	**service:** an activity that helps people
money: coins and paper bills used to buy things	**shelter:** a safe place to stay
need: must have	**shopping list:** things someone will buy

sort: to put things that are alike in groups

spend: to use money to buy something

stamp: a sticker that shows that you paid money

tip: money to give to a helpful person

total: the cost of items added together

trade: to give something and get something else

want: to wish

work: to do things for money

worth: has the same value as something else

Using Money to Trade

Understanding the Student Perspective

Children start trading things with each other at a young age: they see a sibling or a friend with something that they want, and they offer something in return. Ever since coins came into use 5,000 years ago, traders have been able to exchange goods and services for something of universal value: money.

By the time children are in school, they realize that they can't have everything they want, and that other people may want similar things. Fairness is important to them. However, they must remember that both people have to agree that a trade is fair.

This unit helps students understand that trading involves giving and receiving goods or services that are worth about the same. They can use money in the trade, and both traders should get something they want. The math skills used in this unit include skip counting, addition, and using currency.

Pacing/Lesson Plan

1. Distribute a copy of Making Trades on pages 20 and 21 to each student. Read the story aloud to the class as students follow along. Note that the bold words in the story are defined on page 22.

2. Use the Discussion Questions on page 19 to lead a discussion with the class after reading Making Trades.

3. Distribute a copy of the Words to Know on page 22 to each student. Introduce the vocabulary words, rephrasing or explaining as needed. Then read the directions for the vocabulary practice and have students complete the activity.

4. Distribute a copy of What Things Are Worth on page 23 to each student. Read each item to students and provide support as they complete the activity.

5. Distribute a copy of How Much Money? on page 24 to each student. Make play-money coins or other counters available for students. Read each item to students and provide support as they complete the activity.

6. Distribute a copy of Pam the Plum Picker on page 25 to each student. Make play-money bills or other counters available for students. Read the story and each item to students and provide support as they complete the activity.

7. Have students do the Class Gift-Swap Party activity on page 26. To prepare, make copies of the Gift Cards on pages 27–29 and cut them out. Make sure there is one card per player. Also provide enough $1 play money bills for the activity.

Discussion Questions

Use these questions to lead a discussion with the class after reading the story. You may also wish to add your own questions.

- Have you ever traded with someone? What things did you trade?

- What did Kayten want to trade? *[Purple Treehouse books for Bikes with Wings books]*
  Was this trade fair to both Kayten and Haruto? *[no]*
  Why wasn't it fair? *[Haruto had more books to trade than Kayten did.]*

- Think of something special that you got (a fun toy, a favorite thing to wear, a skateboard, etc.). Would you trade it for anything? If so, what?

- What did Kayten give Haruto at the end of the story? *[four books and $2]*
  Do you think it is easy to trade with money? Why or why not?

 Materials

For word problems on pages 24 and 25:
- play-money coins and bills (see pages 10 and 11)
- counters (optional)

For Class Gift-Swap Party on pages 26–29—each student needs:
- one Gift Card from pages 27–29
- $5 in play money, page 10

 Vocabulary Words

cost	deal	fair
money	trade	worth

Making Trades

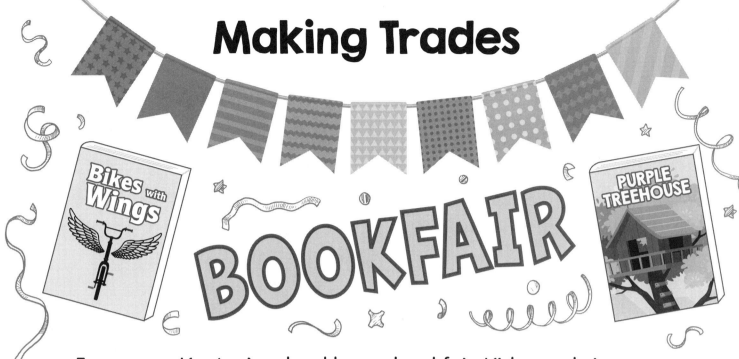

Every year Kayten's school has a bookfair. Kids can bring **money** to buy new books. They can also bring books from home and make a **deal** to **trade** with someone.

Kayten's teacher, Mr. Zahim, told the class, "Remember, kids, the bookfair is tomorrow. Bring money if you want to buy new books. Most books **cost** about $4. If you are going to trade books with someone, make sure the deal is **fair**."

Haruto raised his hand. "How will we know if the deal is fair?" he asked.

"Well," answered Mr. Zahim, "think about what each book is **worth**. That means how much it means to you. For example, your favorite book may be worth a lot to you even if it did not cost much. You may not want to trade it."

Financial Literacy Lessons and Activities • EMC 3121 • © Evan-Moor Corporation

The next day was the bookfair. Kayten had $6. She also brought four <u>Purple Treehouse</u> books. She was hoping to trade with someone who had <u>Bikes with Wings</u> books.

Haruto did not bring any money with him, but he brought six <u>Bikes with Wings</u> books. He wanted to trade with someone.

Kayten saw Haruto holding his books. "Do you want to trade?" Kayten asked.

"Maybe," said Haruto. "What do you have to trade?"

"I have four <u>Purple Treehouse</u> books," said Kayten.

"Well, I have six books. So I'm not sure if that would be fair," said Haruto.

"Okay, how about if I give you my four books and $2. Does that seem fair?"

"It's a deal!" said Haruto.

Name _____

Words to Know

money	coins and paper bills used to buy things
deal	something that you agree to
trade	to give something and get something else
cost	what you have to pay for something
fair	the same for everyone
worth	has the same value as something else

Read the word. Then write it in the sentence. Read the sentence.

money   I use _____ to buy things.

deal   My sister and I made a _____
to share the tablet.

trade   I want to _____ my apple for
an orange.

cost   These toys _____ three dollars.

fair   Let's take turns so it is _____.

worth   My new bike is _____ forty dollars.

Financial Literacy Lessons and Activities • EMC 3121 • © Evan-Moor Corporation

Name _____

What Things Are Worth

Read. Do the items.

1. Pretend that your mom made you a pair of blue mittens. Your friend wants them, but he does not have any money. He asked if you want to trade something for them. Draw a picture or write words to tell what you would do.

I would trade for this:

OR

I would **not** trade them because

_____

_____

_____.

2. Think about one of your favorite things. What would be a fair trade for it? Draw pictures to show.

My favorite thing

I would trade for this:

Name _____

How Much Money?

Read each word problem. Write or draw your answers.

1. Raj has a lemonade stand. He buys 2 lemons from David. The lemons cost 60¢ each. Circle coins to show what he paid.

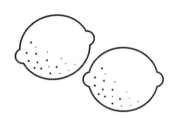

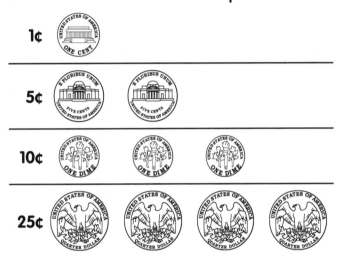

2. David likes toy cars. He buys a new car from Alli. He gave her all the coins below. How much did the car cost?

_____ ¢

3. Alli buys a cup of lemonade from Raj. It costs 75¢. Draw the coins she gave to Raj.

Financial Literacy Lessons and Activities • EMC 3121 • © Evan-Moor Corporation

Pam the Plum Picker

Read about how Pam earns money. Then read each word problem. Write or draw your answers.

Pam's neighbors have lots of plum trees.

Pam picks plum trees for her neighbors. They trade money for Pam's plum-picking service.

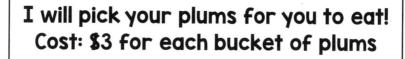

Pam's Plum Picking

I will pick your plums for you to eat!
Cost: $3 for each bucket of plums

1. Pam picked 2 buckets of plums for Mr. Salas. How much did Mr. Salas pay Pam?

$_____

2. Ms. Yi got double the plums that Mr. Salas got. How much did Ms. Yi pay?

$_____

3. Mr. Hays paid $9. Draw the buckets that Pam filled.

Class Gift-Swap Party

Tell the class to pretend that they are having a party, and each student will receive a pretend gift. They will each get a card showing their pretend gift. They will have a chance to trade for a different gift.

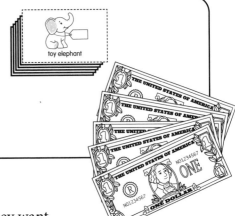

SET-UP

- Get into groups of about 8 players. Sit in a circle.

- Gather materials: play money in $1s; Gift Cards on pages 27–29

- Give $5 of play money and one Gift Card to each player.

PLAY

The object of the game is to trade gifts until all players have something they want.

Have players look at their card. One at a time, have each player tell his or her group what gift he or she has.

On each turn, the player says either "I'll keep my gift" or "I want to trade my gift for another" and states which one. The owner of the other gift says "yes," "no," or "I'll trade for money."

- If "yes," the players trade Gift Cards, and it is the next player's turn.

- If "no," the players keep their Gift Cards, and it is the next player's turn.

- If "I'll trade for money," the players discuss a price. If they agree on a price, they trade money for the Gift Card. The first player keeps both Gift Cards.

Play continues until all players are happy with what they have or until a time limit set by the teacher has been reached.

EXAMPLE

If needed, the teacher can demonstrate play with a student similar to the following:

Teacher:	I want to trade my toy elephant for the book.
Player with book:	I'll trade for money.
Teacher:	Okay, I'll give you $3.
Player:	I want $4.
Teacher:	It's a deal! *(Player gives teacher the Gift Card, teacher gives player $4)*

Gift Cards

toy elephant

toy bear

basketball

paint and brushes

drum

toy plane

book

necklace

Gift Cards

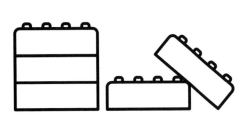

toy bricks

toy car

soccer ball

doll

baseball mitt

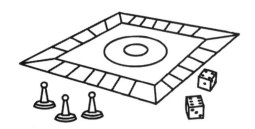

board game

stickers

action figure

Using Money to Trade

Gift Cards

baseball bat

toy robot

puzzle

sled

yo-yo

toy dinosaur

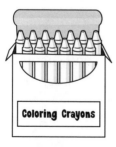

crayons

bubbles

Buying Groceries

Understanding the Student Perspective

Children often go to the grocery store with their parents. Some people write a list before they go to the store. The list may have things they need and things they want. Some people may be able to buy only what they need; they may not have enough money to buy everything they want. This is a concept that is often difficult for children to understand. Learning about the cost of goods and money may help make this concept more meaningful to children.

This unit helps students understand that people have to make choices about what to buy. These choices sometimes depend on how much money they have available to spend. The math skills used in this unit include addition, subtraction, and using currency.

Pacing/Lesson Plan

1. Distribute a copy of Family Shopping Day on pages 32 and 33 to each student. Read the story aloud to the class as students follow along. Note that the bold words in the story are defined on page 34.

2. Use the Discussion Questions on page 31 to lead a discussion with the class after reading Family Shopping Day.

3. Distribute a copy of the Words to Know on page 34 to each student. Introduce the vocabulary words, rephrasing or explaining as needed. Then read the directions for the vocabulary practice and have students complete the activity.

4. Distribute a copy of What Would You Buy? on page 35 to each student. Read each item to students and provide support as they complete the activity.

5. Distribute a copy of Dan Bakes Cookies on page 36 to each student. Make play-money bills or other counters available for students. Read each item to students and provide support as they complete the activity.

6. Distribute a copy of Sachi's Birthday on page 37 to each student. Make play-money bills or other counters available for students. Read each item to students and provide support as they complete the activity.

7. Have students do the Let's Get Lunch activity on page 38. To prepare, make a copy of the Price List on page 39. Cut the items apart and place them around the room. Make copies of the Shopping List on page 40 and the Lunch Foods on page 41 for each pair of students. Gather the other needed materials.

Discussion Questions

Use these questions to lead a discussion with the class after reading the story. You may also wish to add your own questions.

- On Family Shopping Day, what did Rosa and Marga get to do? *[They got to be customers and shop for groceries.]*

- Why could Rosa buy something she wanted? *[She had money left over after she bought everything she needed.]*

- Why couldn't Marga buy a pack of gum and muffins? *[She didn't have money left over after she bought the things on her list.]*

- Have you ever gone grocery shopping with someone? Tell what happened.

- What is something you **need** from the store? What is something you **want** from the store?

 Materials

For word problems on pages 36 and 37:
- play-money bills (see page 10)
- counters (optional)

For Let's Get Lunch on pages 38–41—each pair of students needs:
- Shopping List, page 40
- Lunch Foods, page 41
- $20 in play money
- a pencil

optional:
- a paper plate for each student
- crayons
- scissors
- glue

 Vocabulary Words

cashier	customer	need
shopping list	total	want

Family Shopping Day

Today Rosa and Marga get to be **customers**! The whole family is at the grocery store for Family Shopping Day. They are shopping for things they **need**. Mom and Dad give each child $20 before they go into the store.

Rosa and Marga each made a **shopping list**.

Rosa's shopping list

- apples
- carrots
- milk
- bread
- eggs

Marga's shopping list

- crackers
- grape juice
- cheese
- chicken
- butter

Rosa gets to shop first. She finds a cart.

"I think I will get these cookies," Rosa says.

"Is that on your list?" asks Dad.

Rosa looks at her list. She says "no." She puts the cookies back. Then she finds apples, carrots, milk, bread, and eggs. She puts them in her cart.

She takes the cart to the checkout line. The **cashier** adds up the prices. He says, "Your **total** is $15."

Rosa counts out $15. She says, "I have $5 left!"

Dad says, "You got everything you need from your list. Now you can get something you **want**!" Rosa gets a pack of gum and the cookies she wanted.

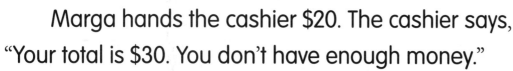

"My turn!" says Marga. "I can push the cart. Let's go!"

Marga gets all the food on her list. She also gets a pack of gum and muffins.

Marga hands the cashier $20. The cashier says, "Your total is $30. You don't have enough money."

Mom asks, "Is it more important to get what you want or what you need?"

"I think it is more important to get what I need. We need the things on my list. I don't need gum or muffins," Marga tells the cashier sadly.

On the way home, Rosa drops something into Marga's lap. "Here, Marga."

Marga looks down and sees a pack of gum.

"I know you wanted some gum," says Rosa. "I don't need it. You can have it!"

Name _____

Words to Know

customer	a person who shops at a store
need	must have
shopping list	things someone will buy
cashier	a person who takes money at a store
total	the cost of items added together
want	to wish

Read the word. Then write it in the sentence. Read the sentence.

customer The _____ pays for the food.

need I _____ a new hat.

shopping list Corn is on my _____.

cashier The _____ takes my money.

total The _____ is $26.

want They _____ to buy candy.

Financial Literacy Lessons and Activities • EMC 3121 • © Evan-Moor Corporation

Name _____

What Would You Buy?

Read. Draw to finish the items.

1. If you go to the grocery store…

Draw 3 things that you **need** to put in your shopping cart. 	Draw 3 things that you **want** to put in your shopping cart. 

2. Oh no! You only have enough money to buy one thing. Choose one thing and circle it. Tell why you chose it.

_____

_____

_____

Name _____

Dan Bakes Cookies

Read each word problem. Write or draw your answers.

1. Dan goes to the store to get things to make cookies. He needs flour, eggs, and milk.

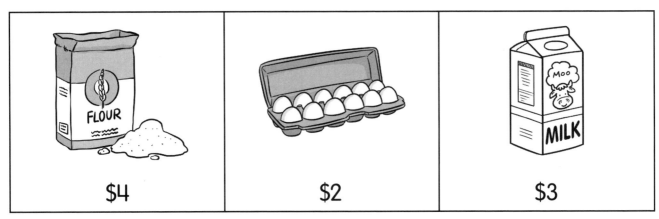

$4	$2	$3

How much will he pay? $_____

2. Dan has $10. He wants to buy some sprinkles for $2. Does he have enough money to buy sprinkles, too? Circle **yes** or **no**.

yes   **no**

3. Dan gives the cashier $10. Circle what the cashier gives back.

Financial Literacy Lessons and Activities • EMC 3121 • © Evan-Moor Corporation

Name _____

Sachi's Birthday

Sachi goes shopping for her birthday. Read about Sachi's shopping trip. Write your answers.

1. Sachi has $40. Look at her shopping list.

Birthday Shopping List			
cake	$10	pizza	$12
ice cream	$4	chips	$3
candles	$1	lemonade	$3

Add the prices. What is the total? $_____

2. Sachi wants some balloons. They cost $6. Does she have enough money left over to buy these? Circle **yes** or **no**.

yes

no

Show how you know.

© Evan-Moor Corporation • EMC 3121 • Financial Literacy Lessons and Activities

Let's Get Lunch

Tell the class that they will pretend to go grocery shopping with a partner. They have $20 to spend. They will buy food for their lunch.

WHAT YOU NEED

- Price List, page 39

- Shopping List, page 40

- Lunch Foods, page 41

- a pencil

- play money (five 1-dollar bills, one 5-dollar bill, and one 10-dollar bill) for each pair of students

Optional:

- paper plates, 1 per student

- crayons

- scissors

- glue

WHAT YOU DO

1. Cut apart the items on the Price List. They are arranged in groups, similar to the sections of a store. The first row of foods contains bakery items; the second row is sandwich fillings; the third row is fruits and vegetables; the last row is cold drinks and desserts. Tape each group of items in different areas around the room.

2. Put students in pairs. Give each pair of students a copy of the Shopping List, the Lunch Foods, and $20 in play money. Have pairs write on the Shopping List the things that they want to buy from the Lunch Foods page. They do not need to fill every line on their list.

3. After all student pairs finish their list, point out the four sections of the store where you have placed the food prices. Have students find the items on their list and write the prices. Next, have them add up the prices and figure out if they have enough money. If they don't, they can change their list.

4. When their lists are ready, they pay you, the cashier, for their food.

5. Optional: After students have paid, they can cut out the items they chose for lunch, color them, and glue them to a paper plate.

Buying Groceries

Price List

bread	(cookie)	Hot Dog Buns Fresh!	BAKED CHIPS
$2	$2	$2	$1
COOKED Ham	Tuna Fish	Peanut Butter	Cheese Slices
$3	$1	$5	$5
Carrots	(apples)	(grapes)	(salad)
$2	$1	$3	$4
water	Chocolate Pudding	Ice Cream 1 Pint	(lemonade)
$2	$2	$2	$1

Shopping List

Item:	Price:
_____	$_____
_____	$_____
_____	$_____
_____	$_____
_____	$_____
_____	$_____
_____	$_____
_____	$_____
_____	$_____
_____	$_____
_____	$_____
_____	$_____
_____	$_____
_____	$_____

Lunch Foods

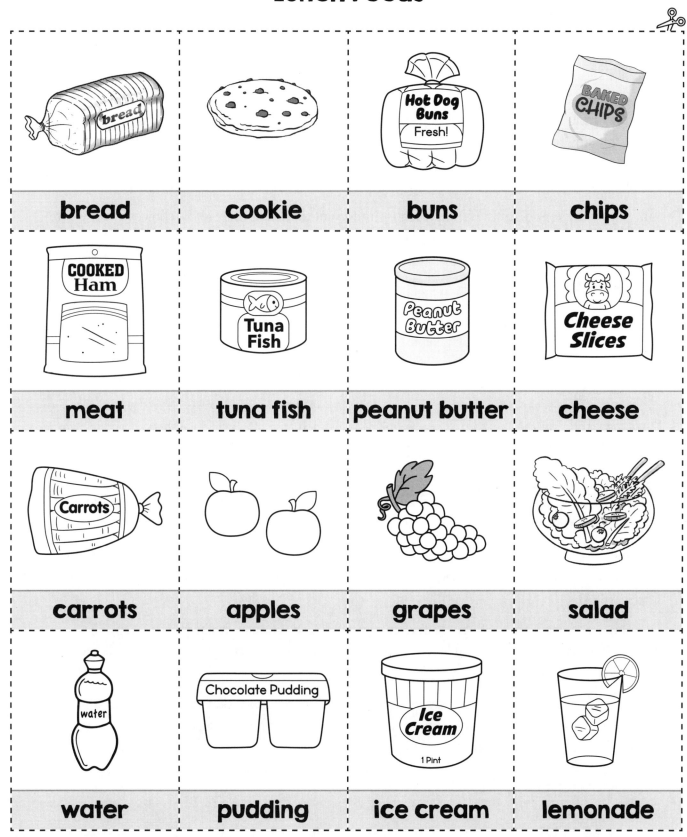

bread	**cookie**	**buns**	**chips**
meat	**tuna fish**	**peanut butter**	**cheese**
carrots	**apples**	**grapes**	**salad**
water	**pudding**	**ice cream**	**lemonade**

Shopping for Clothes

Understanding the Student Perspective

Many children see family members shopping for clothes, and children may be asked to try on clothes in the store to make sure they fit. As with buying groceries, children are just starting to develop a sense of value and worth. Unlike food, which is gone after one use, clothing is generally expected to last longer and be worn many times. How long depends on how fast the child grows and how fast the clothes wear out. Whether clothes shopping is done in person or online, at a clothing store, a thrift store, or a yard sale, it involves making choices about features such as fit, color, warmth, durability, and cost.

This unit helps students distinguish what is most important to them as they make choices about what to buy. The math skills used in this unit include addition, subtraction, and currency.

Pacing/Lesson Plan

1. Distribute a copy of Feature Fishing on pages 44 and 45 to each student. Read the story aloud to the class as students follow along. Note that the bold words in the story are defined on page 46.

2. Use the Discussion Questions on page 43 to lead a discussion with the class after reading Feature Fishing.

3. Distribute a copy of the Words to Know on page 46 to each student. Introduce the vocabulary words, rephrasing or explaining as needed. Then read the directions for the vocabulary practice and have students complete the activity.

4. Distribute a copy of Gone Shopping on page 47 to each student. Read each item to students and provide support as they complete the activity.

5. Distribute a copy of Shopping for Mom on page 48 to each student. Make play-money bills or other counters available for students. Read each item to students and provide support as they complete the activity.

6. Distribute a copy of Jason's Shopping Trip on page 49 to each student. Make play-money bills or other counters available for students. Read each item to students and provide support as they complete the activity.

7. Have students do the Winter Wear activity on page 50. To prepare, make copies of Winter Clothing on page 51, I Can Show My Work on page 52, and Me in the Winter on page 53 for each student. Gather the other needed materials.

Discussion Questions

Use these questions to lead a discussion with the class after reading the story. You may also wish to add your own questions.

- What does Ella need from the store? *[a new winter coat]*
  What game do Ella and her mom play to find a new winter coat? *[Feature Fishing]*
  What features does Ella want her new coat to have? *[to be short, green, and warm; have a zipper and a hood]*

- Have you ever gone shopping for clothes? Tell what happened.

- Have you ever had a hard time finding something you needed when shopping for clothes? Tell what happened.

- Why do Ella and her mom have to play Feature Fishing again tomorrow?
  [Ella's mom needs new snow boots.]
  What are some features that people look for in snow boots (or rain boots)?

 Materials

For word problems on pages 48 and 49:
- play-money bills (see pages 10 and 11)
- counters (optional)

For Winter Wear on pages 50–53—each student needs:
- Winter Clothing, page 51
- I Can Show My Work, page 52
- Me in the Winter, page 53
- $75 in play money (see pages 10 and 11)
- scissors
- glue
- crayons, colored pencils, or markers

 Vocabulary Words

cash register	clerk	department store
feature	product	

Feature Fishing

It is going to snow this week. Ella tries on her old winter coat and snow boots. She wants to make sure they still fit.

"Uh oh! My boots fit, but my coat is too small!" says Ella.

"Let's go shopping for a new one!" says Ella's mom.

Ella and her mom go to the **department store** near their home. They find the part of the store that sells clothing **products**. Mom asks, "Do you want to play a game to find a new coat?"

"Yes, I want to play!" says Ella.

"It's called **Feature** Fishing. You make a list of the features that you want your coat to have. Then we look for a coat that matches your list," Mom explains.

Ella thinks. Then she makes a list. "That's a great list, Ella," says Mom. "I'm going to add one thing. The coat should cost $20 or less."

○ My winter coat:
short
green
warm and fuzzy
○ hood
zipper
no buttons
○

"Okay, let's play!" says Ella.

Ella looks at some coats. She grabs a green coat. "What do you think, Mom?"

"Let's look at your list and see if it matches. Is it short and green?" asks Mom.

"It is green. But it's long, not short. I'll keep looking," says Ella.

Ella finds another coat. "How about this one?" Ella asks. "It's green and short!" Then she looks sad. "Oh, it has buttons. I want a zipper." Ella puts the coat back.

They can't find a coat that matches Ella's list. They ask a **clerk** for help.

The clerk takes them to the front of the store. He shows them a short green fuzzy coat with a hood and a zipper.

"That's perfect!" says Ella, clapping her hands.

"Just one more thing! How much does it cost?" asks Mom. Ella hopes it is less than $20.

The clerk looks at the price tag. "It's $18. Is that okay?"

"Yes!" says Mom. They pay for it at the **cash register**. Ella says, "I love playing Feature Fishing."

Mom says, "Good! We have to play it again soon. My snow boots have a hole in the toe!"

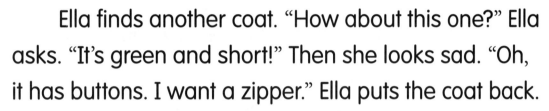

Name _____

Words to Know

department store	a place that sells different kinds of goods
product	something you buy at a store
feature	an important part of something
clerk	someone who works at a store
cash register	a machine that adds prices and holds cash

Read the word. Then write it in the sentence. Read the sentence.

department store This _____ sells toys, clothes, and videos.

product If I need a _____ such as toothpaste, I go to a drug store.

feature A _____ of this shirt is that it has short sleeves.

clerk The _____ helps us find some gloves.

cash register I pay for gum at the _____

_____.

Name _____

Gone Shopping

Pretend that you are going to a clothing store. You will buy a new shirt and a pair of pants. Read the items. Write and draw to answer.

Features
color
size
fit
warmth
cost

1. Write 3 features your shirt should have. Draw a picture.

_____

_____

_____

2. Write 3 features your pants should have. Draw a picture.

_____

_____

_____

Name _____

Shopping for Mom

Hannah and her dad go shopping for her mom. Read each word problem. Write or draw your answers.

1. Hannah picks out shoes and a necklace for her mom. She paid $22. The shoes cost $17. How much does the necklace cost?

$ _____

2. The shoes do not fit her mom. Hannah and her dad take them back to the store. The clerk gives them the money they paid for the shoes. Circle the item or items Hannah could buy with this money.

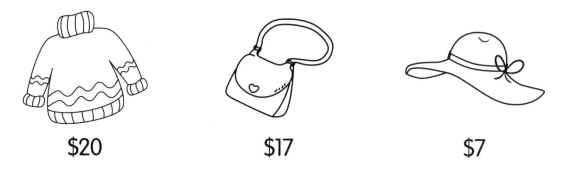

$20 $17 $7

3. Circle the money that Hannah would give to the clerk to buy the sweater.

Financial Literacy Lessons and Activities • EMC 3121 • © Evan-Moor Corporation

Name _____

Jason's Shopping Trip

Jason needs new clothes for school. Look at the clothes.
Then read each word problem. Write or draw your answers.

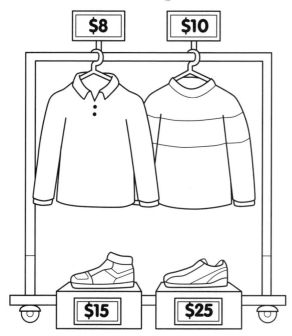

1. Jason needs one shirt, one pair of pants, and one pair
of shoes. His parents gave him $45.

Circle what he could buy.

How much do they cost? $_____

2. Jason wants to buy a cap and a belt to wear with his new
clothes. He has saved $15. Can he buy the cap, the belt,
or both? Circle what he can buy.

$8 $7

Winter Wear

Tell the class to pretend that they will go shopping for winter clothes. They will each get $75.

WHAT YOU NEED

- Winter Clothing, page 51
- I Can Show My Work, page 52
- Me in the Winter, page 53
- play money ($75 for each student)

- scissors
- glue
- crayons, colored pencils, or markers

WHAT YOU DO

1. Distribute play money, a copy of Winter Clothing, and a copy of I Can Show My Work to each student.

2. Tell students to choose what winter clothes they want to buy. They have $75.
   They do not have to spend all of it. They can keep track of their spending two ways:

   - **play money:** they can count out the play money that they are spending as they choose each item

   - **I Can Show My Work:** they can use the sheet as scratch paper, writing the prices and adding to find their total

3. Distribute a copy of Me in the Winter to each student. Have students cut out and glue the clothing items that they chose onto the body shape. Have them use crayons, colored pencils, or markers to add their face and hair and to color their clothes.

EXAMPLE

Show the class an example of a completed project.

Shopping for Clothes

Winter Clothing

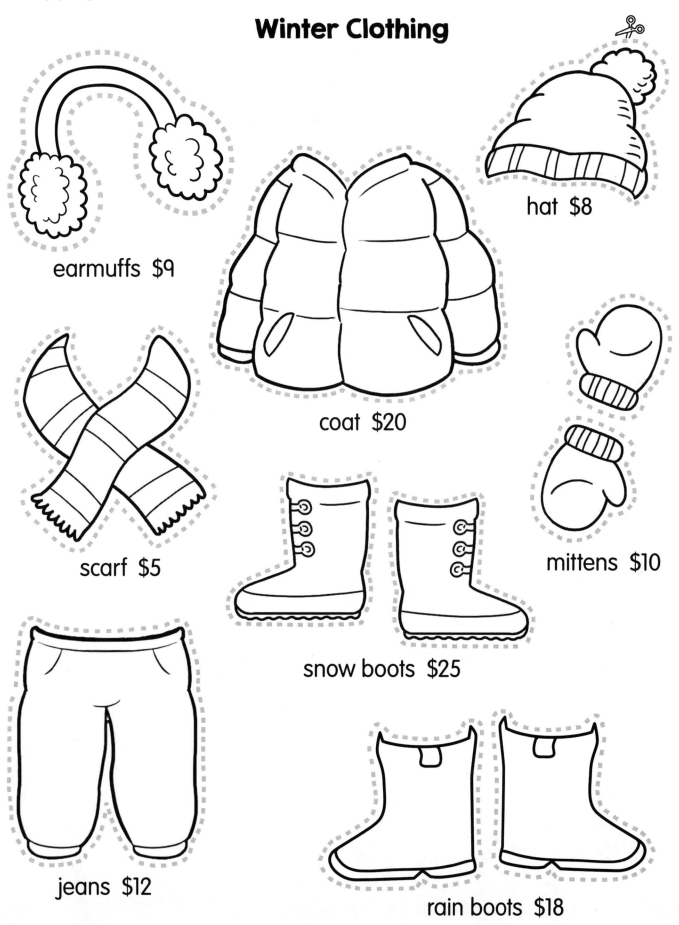

earmuffs $9

coat $20

hat $8

scarf $5

snow boots $25

mittens $10

jeans $12

rain boots $18

Name _____

I Can Show My Work

My total: $_____

Financial Literacy Lessons and Activities • EMC 3121 • © Evan-Moor Corporation

Name _____

Me in the Winter

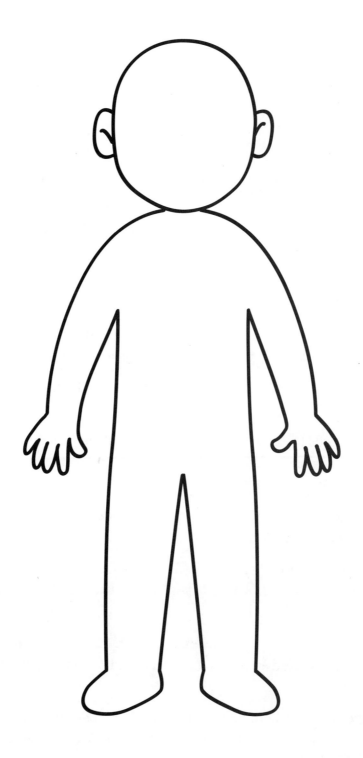

© Evan-Moor Corporation • EMC 3121 • Financial Literacy Lessons and Activities

Earning Money in Your Family

 Understanding the Student Perspective

Children rarely have a sense of how much things cost since parents provide everything for them from the time they are born. They may have even less sense of the effort needed to afford what parents buy. As children get older, they often want certain things. Earning money and then spending it helps them understand its value. If they know how hard they worked to earn money, they may put more thought into how they use it and may better appreciate gifts.

Children often have opportunities to receive money from family members. Money given as a gift or earned from chores helps develop skills in saving and making spending decisions.

This unit helps students understand that money has value and make connections between working and buying something they want. The math skills used in this unit include skip counting, addition, subtraction, and using currency.

 Pacing/Lesson Plan

1. Distribute a copy of The Chore Chart on pages 56 and 57 to each student. Read the story aloud to the class as students follow along. Note that the bold words in the story are defined on page 58.

2. Use the Discussion Questions on page 55 to lead a discussion with the class after reading The Chore Chart.

3. Distribute a copy of the Words to Know on page 58 to each student. Introduce the vocabulary words, rephrasing or explaining as needed. Then read the directions for the vocabulary practice and have students complete the activity.

4. Distribute a copy of A Choice of Chores on page 59 to each student. Read each item to students and provide support as they complete the activity.

5. Distribute a copy of Earn and Buy on page 60 to each student. Make play-money bills or other counters available for students. Read each item to students and provide support as they complete the activity.

6. Distribute a copy of Surprise Gifts on page 61 to each student. Make play-money bills or other counters available for students. Read each item to students and provide support as they complete the activity.

7. Have students play the Guess My Chore game on page 62. To prepare, make a copy of the Pay Envelopes on page 63 for each pair of students and cut them out. Make a copy of The Bank on page 64 and a set of Chore Cards on page 65 for each pair of students. Cut out the cards.

Discussion Questions

Use these questions to lead a discussion with the class after reading the story. You may also wish to add your own questions.

- Why are Carter and Cami excited to do their chores? *[They want to earn more money to buy a new game.]*
  Do they have enough money to buy the game after doing their chores? *[no]*

- Do you have chores at home? If you do, what are they?

- Do you get an allowance?

- Do Carter and Cami get to buy the game at the end of the story? *[yes]*
  How did they get enough money to buy the game? *[Aunt Jen gave Cami money for her birthday. Added to their allowance, it gave them enough money to buy the game.]*

 Materials

For word problems on pages 60 and 61:
- play-money bills (see pages 10 and 11)
- counters (optional)

For Guess My Chore on pages 62–65—each pair needs:
- two Pay Envelopes, page 63
- The Bank, page 64
- a set of Chore Cards, page 65
- $30 in play money in $1s

 Vocabulary Words

allowance	chore	earn
gift	work	

Name _____

The Chore Chart

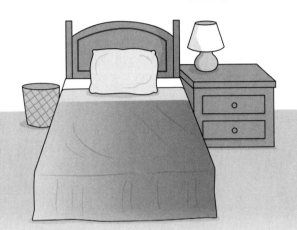

It's Game Day! Carter and Cami are excited to **work** and **earn** money. They are saving money to buy a new game. They hope to have enough money today.

They need $30. Carter counts the money in his envelope. He says, "I have $7, Cami."

"I have $6," says Cami. "Your $7 plus my $6 is $13. We still need $17 more to buy the game we want."

"Let's look at the **chore** chart," says Carter. "What chores can we do to earn $17?"

"Oh no! Even if we do all the chores, we still won't have enough money to buy the game," says Carter.

Chore Chart

Chore	Pay
brush the dog	$1
set the table	$2
make my bed	$2
clean my room	$3

"Right," says Cami. "We will have only $26. I guess we will have to buy the game next week when we get our **allowance** again."

Cami brushes the dog. Carter sets the table. Then they both make their beds and clean their rooms. Mom pays them. They both put their money in their envelopes.

Later, they hear Mom yell from downstairs, "Cami, come here!"

Cami and Carter run down the steps. "This card just came in the mail from Aunt Jen." She hands it to Cami. Cami opens it.

"It's an early birthday **gift**. She sent me $5," Cami says. "Carter, do you know what this means?"

"Let's go buy the game!" says Carter.

Name _____

Words to Know

work	to do things for money
earn	to get money for doing a job
chore	a small job done at home
allowance	money parents give to children each week
gift	something given to someone

Read the word. Then write it in the sentence. Read the sentence.

work   I help my mom _____ in
              the garden.

earn   She will _____ money for
              doing her chores.

chores   My _____ are to feed and
              walk the dog.

allowance He saves his _____
              to buy a new bike.

gift   Darrell gave me a _____
              for my birthday.

A Choice of Chores

Read. Do the items.

1. Pretend that you can earn $5 for doing two chores.
Choose two chores and circle them.

clean my room

bring in the mail

dust the tables

feed the pet

dry the dishes

make lunch

2. What is another chore you could do to earn money?
Draw a picture.

Name _____

Earn and Buy

Pablo likes to earn money.
Look at his chore chart.
Read each word problem.
Write or draw your answers.

Pablo's Chore Chart

Chore	Pay
dust the tables	$1
walk the dog	$2
water the garden	$4
clean my room	$5

1. Pablo has $5. He wants to earn money to buy his sister a ring. Look at his chore chart. What chore or chores can he do to buy the ring?

2. Pablo walked the dog three times. He dusted two times. He cleaned his room once. Circle the items Pablo could buy.

Financial Literacy Lessons and Activities • EMC 3121 • © Evan-Moor Corporation

Name _____

Surprise Gifts

Read about how Jade earns money. Then read each word problem. Write or draw your answers.

1. Some of Jade's family lives far away. For her birthday, they send her cards with money inside.

How much money did Jade get in gifts? $_____

2. Grandma sends Jade a book for her birthday. Jade already has that book. She takes it back to the store and gets $12 back. Draw three different ways to show $12.

Guess My Chore

Tell the class that they will play a game called Guess My Chore with a classmate.

SET-UP

- Put students in pairs.

- Gather materials: Each pair needs play money in $1s totaling $30; two Pay Envelopes on page 63, The Bank on page 64, and a set of Chore Cards on page 65.

- Have each pair of students place the stack the Chore Cards facedown in between them. Have them place The Bank in between them and place all play money on top of it. Give each student a Pay Envelope. Students use their own Pay Envelope to stack the money they earn.

PLAY

The object of the game is to earn the most money by acting out chores.

On each turn, one player is the "actor" and the other is the "guesser." The actor takes a chore card. The actor should act out whatever chore is shown on the card. The guesser watches carefully and can make three guesses. The actor can change or refine his or her actions as needed but may not speak except to say "yes" or "no."

- If the guesser is correct, the actor earns the amount shown on the card. The actor takes the money from the bank and puts it on his or her Pay Envelope.

- If the guesser doesn't guess correctly in three tries, the actor tells the guesser what the chore was but does not earn any money.

Players take turns acting out chores until all cards are used or the teacher stops the game.

Have all students count their money. The player in each pair with the most money wins the game.

EXAMPLE

If needed, the teacher can demonstrate how to play.

- The teacher draws a card and acts out what is on the card.

- Have all students try to guess what chore the teacher is acting out.

- If a student guesses correctly, the teacher takes the amount shown on the card from one pair's bank and places it on an envelope. Then return the money to the students' bank.

- If no student guesses correctly, the teacher shows the action again and explains how it shows the chore.

Pay Envelopes

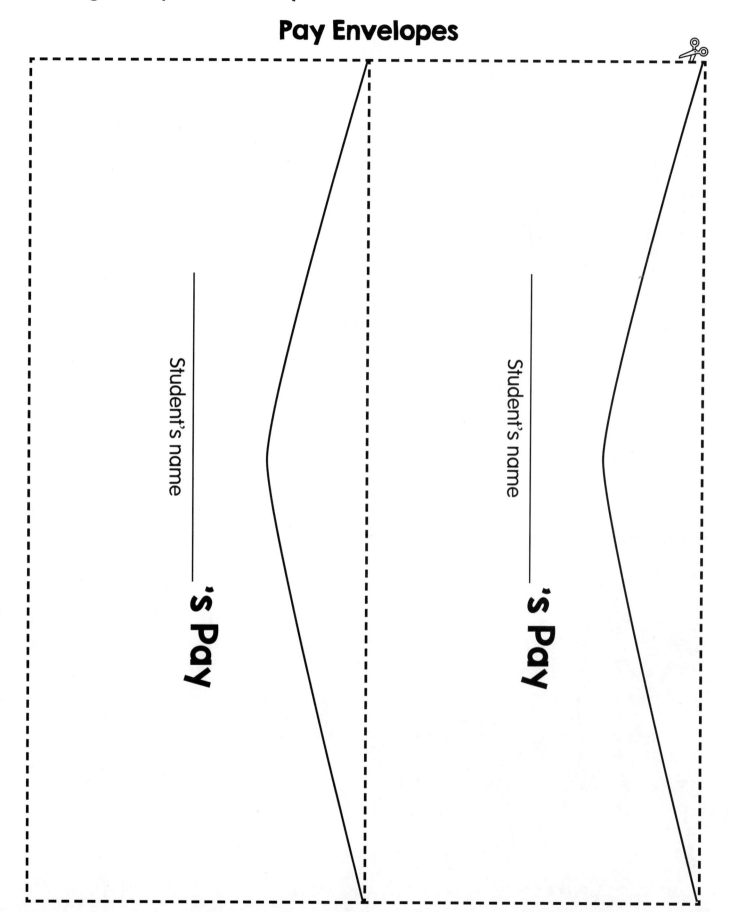

Student's name

's Pay

Student's name

's Pay

© Evan-Moor Corporation • EMC 3121 • Financial Literacy Lessons and Activities

The Bank

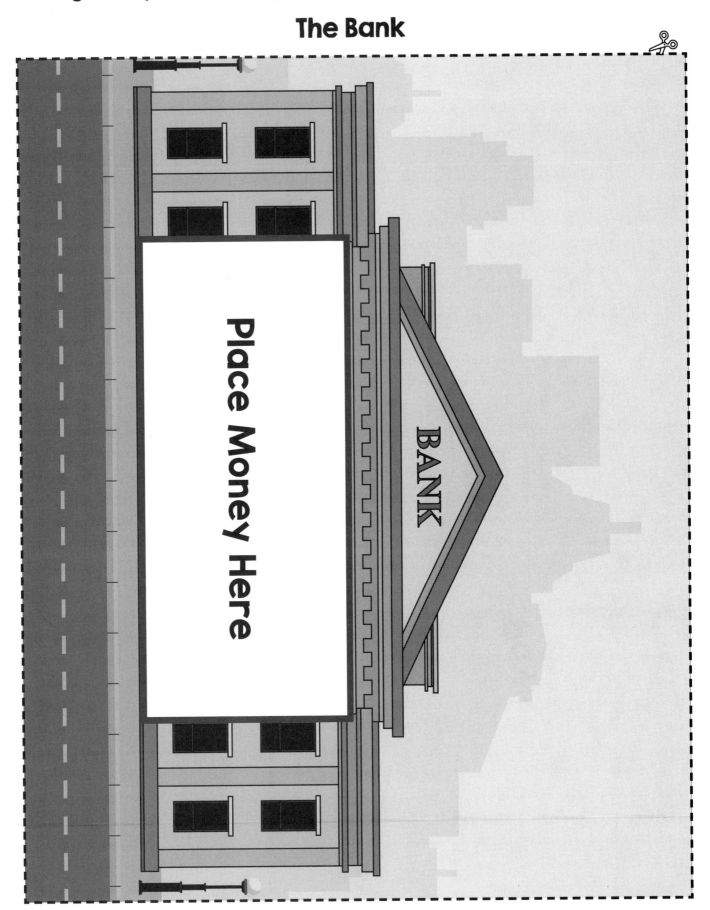

Place Money Here

BANK

Financial Literacy Lessons and Activities • EMC 3121 • © Evan-Moor Corporation

Earning Money in Your Family

Chore Cards

$2 dust	$1 clear the table	$4 clean my room
$3 walk the dog	$2 set the table	$3 take out the trash
$4 pick vegetables	$2 put away laundry	$2 feed the fish
$3 make my bed	$1 wipe off the sink	$3 water plants

Saving Money

Understanding the Student Perspective

Children may have some experience with both using money and saving money at a young age. They might eat a cookie now or save it to eat after lunch. They might save a favorite book for bedtime. They might spend some money now and save some to use later. If children want to buy something that costs more than they have, they may not realize that they can continue adding to their money until they have enough to buy it. Saving small amounts of money lets them buy a larger item. Setting a goal and making a plan to reach the goal can help people save enough to buy things they can't afford right now.

This unit helps students understand that saving comes from money you receive that you don't spend. People save to buy something in the future. Money can be saved in a bank or at home in a special place. The math skills used in this unit include skip counting, addition, subtraction, and using currency.

Pacing/Lesson Plan

1. Distribute a copy of The Savings Plan on pages 68 and 69 to each student. Read the story aloud to the class as students follow along. Note that the bold words in the story are defined on page 70.

2. Use the Discussion Questions on page 67 to lead a discussion with the class after reading The Savings Plan.

3. Distribute a copy of the Words to Know on page 70 to each student. Introduce the vocabulary words, rephrasing or explaining as needed. Then read the directions for the vocabulary practice and have students complete the activity.

4. Distribute a copy of Make a Plan on page 71 to each student. Read each item to students and provide support as they complete the activity.

5. Distribute a copy of Let's Work Together on page 72 to each student. Make play-money bills or other counters available for students. Read each item to students and provide support as they complete the activity.

6. Distribute a copy of Number Trains on page 73 to each student. Make play-money bills or other counters available for students. Read the story and each item to students and provide support as they complete the activity.

7. Have students do the My Savings Jar activity on page 74. To prepare, make copies of Draw a Picture on page 75, Make a Plan on page 76, and Savings Jar Label Cutout on page 77 for each student. Gather the other needed materials.

Discussion Questions

Use these questions to lead a discussion with the class after reading the story. You may also wish to add your own questions.

- Have you ever saved your money for something? What did you save for?

- Why did Ashley save her money? *[to buy a dinosaur at the toy store]*
  Why didn't Owen save his money? *[He didn't know how.]*
  How did Owen feel when he could not buy the dinosaur? What did he learn? *[He was disappointed, but he learned that he could save his money and buy a dinosaur if he made a goal and a plan.]*

- Think of something you would like to buy. Would it be worth it to spend time saving your money?

- How did Ashley get the money she saved? *[doing chores]*

- Do you think it is easy to save money? How does making a plan help?

 Materials

For word problems on pages 72 and 73:
- play-money bills (see pages 10 and 11)
- counters (optional)

For My Savings Jar activity—each student needs:
- Draw a Picture, page 75
- Make a Plan, page 76
- Savings Jar Label Cutout, page 77
- a jar
- crayons
- scissors
- glue

 Vocabulary Words

bank	cash	future
goal	plan	

Name _____

The Savings Plan

Ashley and Owen can't wait until Friday. Their mom is taking them to the toy store to spend their money. They each get paid $5 **cash**, or money, each month for doing chores.

Owen likes to spend his cash right away. On Monday, he bought a pencil and a sticker from the school store. On Tuesday, he bought a candy bar from the grocery store. On Wednesday, he bought his dog a treat at the pet store. He has only $1 left, and he can't wait to spend it on Friday.

Ashley likes spending her cash, too. But she does not spend it right away. She likes to save her money. She saves it in the **bank**. She has a **plan** to use it.

Mom took her there on Thursday. "Are you putting your chore money in the bank again, Ashley?" asked Mom.

"No," said Ashley, "I am taking some out. I reached my **goal**."

"What is your goal?" Mom asked.

"It's a secret!" Ashley said. "You will see on Friday!"

After school on Friday, Mom took Ashley and Owen to the toy store. Ashley picked up a large stuffed dinosaur and went to pay. Owen thought the dinosaur was great. He got one, too.

The toy store worker said, "This dinosaur costs $10."

Ashley counted out her money. "Here you go! I have $10!"

"I don't have enough for a dinosaur," said Owen.

Ashley said, "You need to save to buy big things."

"I won't get anything today," Owen said. "I'll save $1 each month. I will buy a dinosaur when I have $10."

"That's great, Owen. You have made a plan for the **future**," Ashley said. "Now let's go do our chores so we can make some more money!"

Name _____

Words to Know

cash	money, coins and paper bills
bank	a place you can keep your money safe
plan	steps to follow to reach a goal
goal	a plan to save money for something
future	a time next week, next month, or next year

Read the word. Then write it in the sentence. Read the sentence.

cash   I use _____ to buy candy at the store.

bank   I keep my money in the _____.

plan   Let's make a _____ to save our money.

goal   My _____ is to save $10 to buy a toy.

future   I can buy a bike some day in the _____.

Financial Literacy Lessons and Activities • EMC 3121 • © Evan-Moor Corporation

Name _____

Make a Plan

Read. Answer the questions.

1. Pretend that you are at a toy store. You have $5. What will you do? Fill in the circle.

   ○ I will buy   for $5 now.

   ○ I will buy for $5 now.

   ○ I will save my money to buy for $30 in the future.

   I will do this because _____

   _____

   _____.

2. You want to buy your friend a birthday gift. The gift costs $10. How can you save $10?

   I will _____

   _____

   _____.

© Evan-Moor Corporation • EMC 3121 • Financial Literacy Lessons and Activities

Saving Money

Name _____

Let's Work Together

Read each word problem. Write your answers.

Ebony and Idi decided to save their money to buy a new game. It costs $30.

1. Ebony has $2. Then she gets $5 for walking her friend's dog. How much money does she have now?

   $_____

2. Idi counted the money he has saved. How much money does he have?

   $_____

3. Ebony and Idi added their money together. How much do they have?

   $_____

4. The game costs $30. How much more do they need to buy the new game?

   $_____

Financial Literacy Lessons and Activities • EMC 3121 • © Evan-Moor Corporation

Name _____

Number Trains

Look at the number trains. Skip count to fill in the missing numbers.
Then read each word problem. Write your answers.

1. Jasmine saved $20 to ride a train.

How many times can she ride Train 1? _____ times

How many times can she ride Train 2? _____ times

2. Abdul wants to ride Train 2. He has $3.
How much more does Abdul need to
save to ride the train? $ _____

My Savings Jar

Tell the class that they will make their own savings jar. They will choose something to save for, create a goal, and make a plan to meet the goal.

WHAT YOU NEED

- Draw a Picture, page 75
- Make a Plan, page 76
- Savings Jar Label Cutout, page 77
- a jar for each student

- crayons
- scissors
- glue

WHAT YOU DO

1. Distribute a copy of Draw a Picture to each student. Have students complete it.

2. Distribute a copy of Make a Plan to each student. Have students complete it.

3. Distribute a copy of Savings Jar Label Cutout to each student. Have students write their name, their goal, and what they want to buy in the blanks and decorate their label with crayons.

4. Have students cut the label out and glue it to their jar.

5. Have students share their goals, plans, and jars with the class.

6. Have students take their jars home so they can save their money.

EXAMPLE

If needed, provide the following examples of the types of things you can save for:

- a toy
- candy or other treat
- a gift for someone else
- something you have wanted for a long time
- something you want to do that costs money

Name _____

Draw a Picture

1. I want to save my money for _____.

2. Draw a picture of it.

Name _____

Make a Plan

Make a plan to save money to meet your goal. Here are some words to help. Write your plan below.

future   cash   work   money   coins   help   time

Here are 3 ways that I can meet my goal:

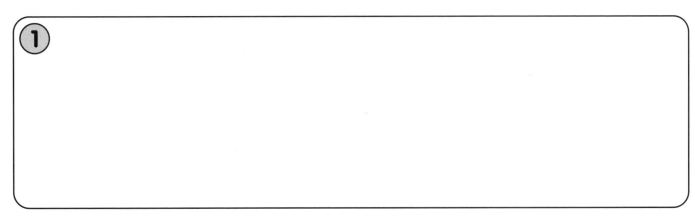

Financial Literacy Lessons and Activities • EMC 3121 • © Evan-Moor Corporation

Savings Jar Label Cutout

_____'s

Savings Jar

My savings goal is $_____

to buy _____.

Paying at a Restaurant

 Understanding the Student Perspective

Children may have noticed that when a meal is served at home, their choices may be limited. One or both parents are busy preparing the meal and then cleaning up afterward. At a restaurant, there are more food choices, and children have more time with their parents. While children may know that parents pay to eat out, they may not notice how it is different from paying in a store. They also might not realize that the cost of a restaurant meal is usually more than a home-cooked meal since diners are also paying for the services involved (cooking, serving, cleaning).

This unit helps students understand some differences between eating at home and eating at a restaurant. The math skills used in this unit include addition, subtraction, and using currency.

 Pacing/Lesson Plan

1. Distribute a copy of Family Night Out on pages 80 and 81 to each student. Read the story aloud to the class as students follow along. Note that the bold words in the story are defined on page 82.

2. Use the Discussion Questions on page 79 to lead a discussion with the class after reading Family Night Out.

3. Distribute a copy of the Words to Know on page 82 to each student. Introduce the vocabulary words, rephrasing or explaining as needed. Then read the directions for the vocabulary practice and have students complete the activity.

4. Distribute a copy of Let's Order! on page 83 to each student. Read each item to students and provide support as they complete the activity.

5. Distribute a copy of What's on the Menu? on page 84 to each student. Make play-money coins and bills or other counters available for students. Read each item to students and provide support as they complete the activity.

6. Distribute a copy of Out to Eat on page 85 to each student. Make play-money coins and bills or other counters available for students. Read each item to students and provide support as they complete the activity.

7. Have students do the Let's Play Restaurant! role-play activity on page 86. To prepare, make copies of the Roles on page 87, Menu on page 88, and Order Form and Check on page 89 for each student. Gather the other needed materials.

Discussion Questions

Use these questions to lead a discussion with the class after reading the story. You may also wish to add your own questions.

- Why does Arpie like eating out on Friday nights? *[The whole family is together.]*

- Does your family like to eat out? What restaurants do you go to?

- How is Jing helpful? *[She gives them menus, answers questions, takes their order, brings drinks and food, clears the table, brings the check.]*

- Do you think food costs more money at a restaurant or at a store? Explain.

 Materials

For word problems on pages 84 and 85:
- play-money coins and bills (see pages 10 and 11)
- counters (optional)

For Let's Play Restaurant! on pages 86–89—each student needs:
- Roles, page 87
- Menu, page 88
- Order Form and Check, page 89
- $12 in play money
- a pencil
- paper plates
- scissors
- tape

 Vocabulary Words

check	menu	order
server	tip	

Name _____

Family Night Out

Every Friday night, Arpie's family eats at a restaurant. Arpie likes Friday nights. The whole family is all together. Mom and Dad won't be busy in the kitchen.

Arpie and his family talk about where they want to eat. They decide to go to a new restaurant. They have never been there before.

When they get there, Mom says, "We're here at Mama Ceci's! It will be nice for another mama to cook!" They all go in. A girl says, "Welcome! I'm Jing. I'll be your **server** today." She leads them to a table. Arpie looks at the tables they walk past. Jing hands each person a **menu**.

Arpie asks, "Everyone has a small dish. Can we get more food than that?"

Jing smiled. "Here we serve small plates of food. Your family shares them," she explained. "You can try many things. That way, you don't have to pick just one thing."

"Okay," said Arpie, "but I'm hungry!"

The family looked at the pictures on the menu.

"Everyone can **order** three dishes," said Mom.

Jing came back. They all told her what they wanted. Dad asked her, "Do any of these dishes have clams? I get sick if I eat clams." Jing said that they didn't.

Jing brought everyone a drink. While they waited for their food, everyone talked and laughed.

Then Jing and some other servers came. Each one put two dishes in the middle of the table! "Let me know if you need anything else," Jing said.

"Wow!" Mom said. "Look at all this pretty food! I'm glad I didn't spend all day cooking it."

They passed the plates around. Arpie tried some new foods. He liked most of them. He asked Jing for another drink.

Everyone finished eating. Jing cleaned off the table and brought the **check**. Mom said, "Let's give Jing a big **tip**. She was very helpful!" They paid and went home, happy and full.

Name _____

Words to Know

server	a person who helps people at a restaurant
menu	a list of choices
order	to ask for something you want to eat
check	a paper that tells how much the meals cost
tip	money to give to a helpful person

Read the word. Then write it in the sentence. Read the sentence.

server The _____ gives us our food.

menu The _____ has many good choices.

order I _____ a sandwich and milk.

check The _____ says we owe $20.

tip She left a _____ on the table.

Name _____

Let's Order!

Read. Write and draw to do the items.

1. Pretend that you can order anything you want at a restaurant. What would you order?

Write your order.   Draw a picture.

_____

_____

_____

_____

2. Pretend that you are a server. You bring food to the table. Look at the orders. Draw the food on the plates.

Orders	
Person 1:	**Person 2:**
apple slices	carrot sticks
cheeseburger	slice of pizza

Name _____

What's on the Menu?

Roy goes out to lunch with Papi. Look at the menu. Read each word problem. Write or draw your answers.

1. Roy has $5. Papi has $9. Draw all the money they have.

2. Roy and Papi want to spend all their money. Draw what they could order. Write each price.

Financial Literacy Lessons and Activities • EMC 3121 • © Evan-Moor Corporation

Name _____

Out to Eat

Jada and Lupe went out for lunch.
Read each word problem.
Write or draw your answers.

1. The server gave them a check for the meal. It shows how much each food cost. Write the total cost of their meal on the check.

MILKY WAY
Restaurant

FOOD	PRICE
Spicy ramen	$4
Crispy shrimp	$6
Brown rice	$2
Lemon chicken	$7
Apple juice	$2
Iced tea	$2
Total	

2. Jada gave a tip to their server. She paid $27 in all. How much was the tip? Draw the tip money Jada left.

Let's Play Restaurant!

Tell the class they will work in pairs to do a role-play at a pretend restaurant. One student will be the customer, and one will be the server.

WHAT YOU NEED

- Roles, page 87, cut as indicated
- Menu, page 88
- Order Form and Check, page 89
- play money ($12 per student)
- pencils
- paper plates
- scissors
- tape

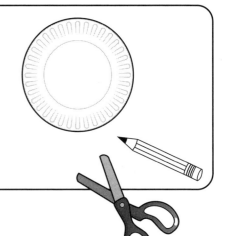

WHAT YOU DO

1. Put the students in pairs. One student is the customer, and the other is the server.

2. Give each **customer** the following: $12 in play money and a copy of the Customer Role.

   Give each **server** the following: a copy of the Menu, a copy of the Order Form and Check, a pencil, and a copy of the Server Role.

   Place the paper plates, scissors, and tape at a station for the servers to use after taking the customer's order.

3. Explain that students will pretend to be in a restaurant during breakfast. Briefly explain each role and point out their Role sheets, which they can look at if they need help.

4. Role-play starts with servers giving a Menu to their customer and letting the customer read it. Then they ask what 3 things the customer would like to eat this morning. Customers point to what they want and tell the server. Have the server write the items and the prices on the Order Form and Check and take the Menu.

5. The servers cut out each ordered item and tape them to a paper plate. Customers can read or do something fun while they wait. Servers bring the plates to the customers. While the customers pretend to eat, the servers add the prices and write the total on the Order Form and Check.

6. The servers give the customers their Order Form and Check. The customers use their play money to give the server the correct total shown on the check plus a tip.

7. Switch roles and repeat.

Paying at a Restaurant

Customer Role

Step 1	Step 2	Step 3	Step 4

Read the menu.	Tell the server what you want.	Eat the food.	Pay for the food and give a tip.

Server Role

Step 1	Step 2	Step 3	Step 4

Give the customer a menu.	Write the order and the prices.	Make and serve the food.	Give the customer the check.

Paying at a Restaurant

Menu

eggs $4

rice and beans $3

juice $1

pancakes $6

fruit cup $2

hot chocolate $3

oatmeal $3

toast $1

milk $2

bacon $4

yogurt $2

coffee $2

miso soup $3

fried potatoes $2

iced tea $2

Financial Literacy Lessons and Activities • EMC 3121 • © Evan-Moor Corporation

Name _____

Order Form and Check

Food Item	Price
1. _____	$ _____
2. _____	$ _____
3. _____	$ _____
Total:	$ _____

Raising Money to Help Others

 Understanding the Student Perspective

Some children may not have experienced or seen hardship. They might assume that everyone in their community has their needs met with the same resources that they have. Some needs are ongoing, such as maintaining food banks, animal shelters, and youth arts programs. Other needs arise following an emergency, such as a house fire, medical treatment, or natural disaster. Communities often respond by fundraising to help those in need.

Help can look different depending on the situation or emergency. Individuals and charities can provide resources for people who need help getting food or housing, have an illness or injury, or are recovering from a natural disaster.

This unit helps students understand how raising money can help provide food, water, shelter, and other necessities to those in need. The math skills used in this unit include skip counting, addition, and using currency.

 Pacing/Lesson Plan

1. Distribute a copy of Help for Charlie on pages 92 and 93 to each student. Read the story aloud to the class as students follow along. Note that the bold words in the story are defined on page 94.

2. Use the Discussion Questions on page 91 to lead a discussion with the class after reading Help for Charlie.

3. Distribute a copy of the Words to Know on page 94 to each student. Introduce the vocabulary words, rephrasing or explaining as needed. Then read the directions for the vocabulary practice and have students complete the activity.

4. Distribute a copy of Ways to Help on page 95 to each student. Read each item to students and provide support as they complete the activity.

5. Distribute a copy of Hungry Firefighters on page 96 to each student. Make play-money bills or other counters available for students. Read each item to students and provide support as they complete the activity.

6. Distribute a copy of Fundraiser for the Farm on page 97 to each student. Make play-money coins and bills or other counters available for students. Read each item to students and provide support as they complete the activity.

7. Have students do the How to Help activity on page 98. To prepare, make copies of Cause Cards on page 99, Our Plan to Help on page 100, and Make a Sign on page 101 for each student. Gather the other needed materials.

Discussion Questions

Use these questions to lead a discussion with the class after reading the story. You may also wish to add your own questions.

- What is Charlie's problem? *[His home was damaged in a flood.]*

- What did Charlie and his family need? *[shelter, clothes, and food]*
  How did Charlie's class help? *[They had a fundraiser to raise money for his family and collect things the family needs.]*

- Have you ever helped someone? How did you help?

- Have you ever given money or worked on a fundraiser? Tell what happened.

 Materials

For word problems on pages 96 and 97:

- play-money coins and bills (see pages 10 and 11)
- counters (optional)

For How to Help on pages 98–101— each pair of students needs:

- a Cause Card from page 99
- Our Plan to Help, page 100
- Make a Sign, page 101
- crayons or markers
- pencils

 Vocabulary Words

damage	donation	flood
fundraiser	shelter	

Help for Charlie

The students in Mrs. Sato's class were talking about the storm before class started.

"Wow, it rained really hard last night!" said Yusuf.

"I know. The thunder was so loud," said Elise.

"Class," said Mrs. Sato, "Charlie will not be in school today. There is a lot of **damage** to his home from the storm."

"Is Charlie okay?" asked Rita.

"Charlie and his family are safe," Mrs. Sato said. "But they will need some help. A **flood** filled their home. They cannot live there right now. It needs to be fixed. They are in a **shelter**. How can we help Charlie and his family?"

Everyone raised their hands at once. "I know! We can have a **fundraiser** to get money for them. I bet all the water ruined their stuff. They will need to buy new things," said Anne.

"They can buy food with the money, too," added Ajit. "Can you take the **donations** to Charlie's family, Mrs. Sato?"

"Of course I can!" Mrs. Sato said.

"I have another idea," Justin said. "Think of anything that Charlie and his family can use, such as toothpaste, snacks, clothing, and toys. Bring them to school tomorrow."

DONATION BOX

Financial Literacy Lessons and Activities • EMC 3121 • © Evan-Moor Corporation

"I have an idea, too," said Thandie. "We can all draw something pretty and bring it to the school art show tonight. We can sell our drawings and give the money to Charlie's family!"

Mrs. Sato said, "These are great ideas. Thandie and Anne, you are in charge of the fundraiser. Justin and Ajit, you gather the donations."

The next morning, Justin and Ajit stood next to a full box. "Look at all these things!" Ajit said.

Mrs. Sato asked about the art show. Thandie held up a handful of bills. Anne said, "We collected $50! This will really help Charlie's family buy what they need."

"Class, I am so proud of you!" said Mrs. Sato. "It is important to show kindness to those in need. I can't wait to take everything to Charlie and his family after school today. He will know that you care about him."

Name _____

Words to Know

damage	harm that is done to something
flood	a lot of water inside a home
shelter	a safe place to stay
fundraiser	a way to gather money for something
donation	money or things given to help people

Read the word. Then write it in the sentence. Read the sentence.

damage   There was _____ to the fence
after the tree fell on it.

flood   The _____ ruined the rug.

shelter   The cat ran up the tree for _____
when the dog chased it.

fundraiser   The _____ will
help us buy food for people who need it.

donation   Please give a _____
to make a new school playground.

Name _____

Ways to Help

Read. Write and draw to do the items.

1. Thandie asked her class to make art to sell as a fundraiser. Think of another fundraiser idea. Tell about it.

_____

_____

2. Think of four things you could donate to a family in need. Draw a picture of each one.

Name _____

Hungry Firefighters

Firefighters work very hard in the heat to put out wildfires. Tim's class gathers food for the firefighters. Read each word problem. Write or draw your answers.

1. Look at the food that Tim buys. How much did he spend?

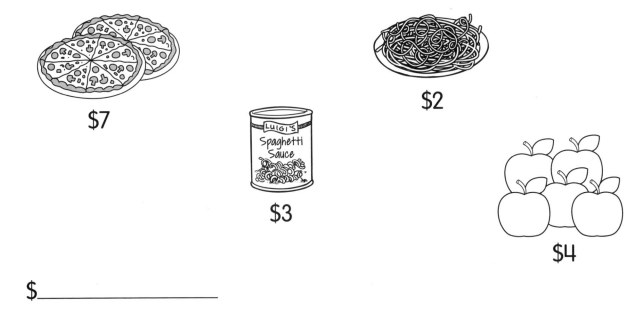

$7

$2

$3

$4

$_____

2. Tim's dad donates some money to help the firefighters eat. Look at the bills. How much money did he give?

$_____

Financial Literacy Lessons and Activities • EMC 3121 • © Evan-Moor Corporation

Name _____

Fundraiser for the Farm

Javien lives on a farm with his family. All their crops have damage from a storm. They can't sell them now. Read each word problem. Write or draw your answers.

1. Javien's school washed cars as a fundraiser. Luisa put each kind of bill in a pile. She counted the number of bills. Skip count to find out how much money is in each pile.

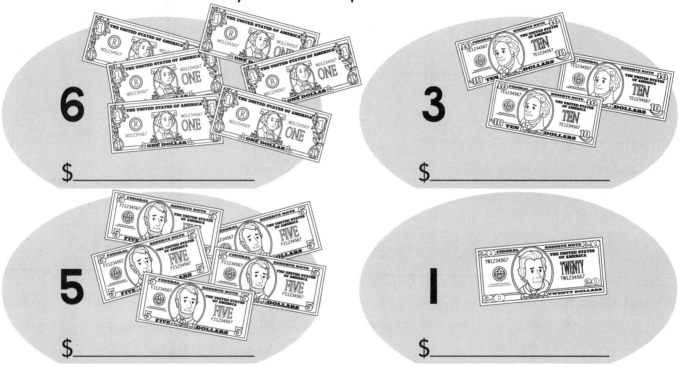

6    $_____

3    $_____

5    $_____

I $_____

2. Javien's community is taking money donations for his family. Count the money from the donation box.

$_____

DONATION

How to Help

Tell the class that they will work in pairs to think of a way to help a group of people in need. Each student will choose a Cause Card that tells a reason for needing help. They will complete the rest of the activity based on this card.

WHAT YOU NEED

- Cause Cards, page 99, cut apart
- Our Plan to Help, page 100
- Make a Sign, page 101
- pencils
- crayons or markers

WHAT YOU DO

1. Put students into pairs. Distribute one Cause Card, a copy of Our Plan to Help, and a copy of Make a Sign to each pair of students.

2. Have students read their Cause Card or read the cards to students. Give them a few minutes to discuss with their partner what they could do to help with the problem on the card.

3. Have students work together to answer the questions on Our Plan to Help.

4. Have students make a sign based on their plan. The sign should make people want to help. Tell students it can include pictures, words, or both. It should tell people about their fundraiser or donation box. Have students draw their signs on the Make a Sign page and share their signs with the class.

BONUS

Have the class brainstorm needs within the school or community. Have students work together to create a plan to raise money or collect items that could help a person or group of people in need.

Raising Money to Help Others

Cause Cards

A family's home is flooded.

A tree fell on a family's house in a storm.

Children in the hospital have no toys to play with.

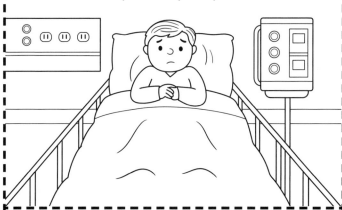

These lost pets need homes.

Firefighters need help when they work many hours.

Children can't play on the broken swings at the park.

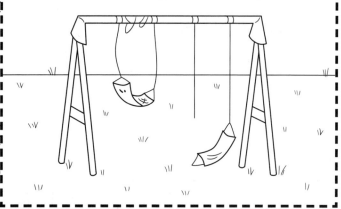

Name _____

Our Plan to Help

Look at your Cause Card. Answer the questions.

Who needs help?

_____

Why do they need help?

_____

_____

What can you do to help?

_____

_____

_____

_____

How will this help them?

_____

_____

_____

Financial Literacy Lessons and Activities • EMC 3121 • © Evan-Moor Corporation

Name _____

Make a Sign

Draw or write to make a donation sign for your fundraiser.

Buying and Selling at a Yard Sale

 Understanding the Student Perspective

Yard sales go by many names—garage sales, lawn sales, rummage sales, jumble sales—but they all involve the same thing: people selling used items for a lower price than a store would charge. Children may have seen or gone to yard sales in their neighborhood. Like stores, yard sales offer a variety of items. Unlike at stores in many places, the buyer can try to negotiate the price. A child might be able to afford a used item that he or she could not afford to buy new. However, all sales from a yard sale are final, and the quality of yard sale items varies greatly.

This unit helps students understand that buying used items from a yard sale saves money. Used items cost less than new items. The math skills used in this unit include addition, subtraction, and using currency.

 Pacing/Lesson Plan

1. Distribute a copy of Finding Treasures on pages 104 and 105 to each student. Read the story aloud to the class as students follow along. Note that the bold words in the story are defined on page 106.

2. Use the Discussion Questions on page 103 to lead a discussion with the class after reading Finding Treasures.

3. Distribute a copy of the Words to Know on page 106 to each student. Introduce the vocabulary words, rephrasing or explaining as needed. Then read the directions for the vocabulary practice and have students complete the activity.

4. Distribute a copy of Use Your Cash on page 107 to each student. Read each item to students and provide support as they complete the activity.

5. Distribute a copy of Dev Shops at a Yard Sale on page 108 to each student. Make play-money bills or other counters available for students. Read each item to students and provide support as they complete the activity.

6. Distribute a copy of Shopping for a Bargain on page 109 to each student. Make play-money bills or other counters available for students. Read each item to students and provide support as they complete the activity.

7. Have students do the Come to My Yard Sale activity on page 110. To prepare, make copies of Yard Sale Items Cutouts on page 111, My Yard Sale on page 112, and My Bargains on page 113 for each student. Gather the other needed materials.

Discussion Questions

Use these questions to lead a discussion with the class after reading the story. You may also wish to add your own questions.

- Why did Raven go to a yard sale? *[Her family just moved. She was shopping for things for her room.]* What are some of the things Raven bought? *[beanbag chair, lamp, toy cat, rug]*

- Have you ever been to a yard sale? If you have, tell about what you saw and did.

- How are Raven and her mom going to make the secondhand bookcase look new? *[They will paint it.]*

- What could you do if you wanted to buy a used item that looked old or broken?

 Materials

For word problems on pages 108 and 109:
- play-money bills (see pages 10 and 11)
- counters (optional)

For Come to My Yard Sale on pages 110–113—each student needs:
- Yard Sale Items Cutouts, page 111
- My Yard Sale, page 112
- My Bargains, page 113
- $20 in play money
- crayons
- scissors
- glue or tape
- a pencil

 Vocabulary Words

bargain	cash	deal
for sale	secondhand	spend

Finding Treasures

Raven's family just moved to a new home. Her new neighborhood is having a yard sale today. Raven is excited. She hopes to find stuff for her new bedroom.

Raven puts some **cash** from her savings jar into her pocket. She has $10 to **spend**. Raven and her mom walk to the yard sale. "How are you going to decorate your room?" asks Mom.

"I want everything in my room to be purple!" says Raven.

At the first table, Raven sits in a big purple beanbag chair. "This chair is so comfy!" she says. Raven stands up and looks at the price on the sticker. The chair costs $7. Raven pays for the chair.

"That chair cost a lot, but I think it was worth it," says Raven. Mom picks it up.

"Did you try to make a **deal** for less money?" asks Mom. "If you think a price is high, you can ask to pay less."

"I didn't, but I'll try that," Raven says. She and her mom go to the next table.

Financial Literacy Lessons and Activities • EMC 3121 • © Evan-Moor Corporation

Raven has $3 left to spend. There are a lot of purple things **for sale** at the next table. She chooses a lamp and a purple toy cat. She also gets a small rug.

"How much does all of this cost?" Raven asks.

"How about $6?" says the man behind the table.

Raven looks sad. "I only have $3 left," she says. "Will you sell these things for that much?"

"Okay, since you are new here," he says. "Welcome to the neighborhood!"

"Thank you!" Raven says as she hands her money to the man.

"Wow, Raven! What a **bargain**!" says Mom. "You got some nice treasures!"

"I sure did. I can't wait to set up my room," says Raven.

Raven and her mom carry the items to her room. Mom says, "Surprise!" Raven looks around. She sees a blue **secondhand** bookcase next to her bed.

"Thanks, Mom, but it's blue. I want purple things in my room."

Mom holds up two paintbrushes and a can of purple paint. "Let's get to work!" says Mom.

"This bookcase will be a real treasure!" says Raven.

Name _____

Words to Know

cash	money, coins and paper bills
spend	to use money to buy something
deal	something that you agree to
for sale	can be bought
bargain	a good price for something
secondhand	something that is used

Read the word. Then write it in the sentence. Read the sentence.

cash   Terry pays for the toy with _____.

spend   I _____ my money on paints.

deal   Lee makes a _____ to buy
                  skates.

for sale   The library has old books _____.

bargain   We got a _____ on our new TV.

secondhand   This is a _____ bike.

Financial Literacy Lessons and Activities • EMC 3121 • © Evan-Moor Corporation

Name _____

Use Your Cash

Read. Draw, write, and circle to do the items.

1. Pretend that you are having a yard sale. What are three things you would sell? Draw them and write their names.

_____ _____ _____

2. These tables are at a yard sale. Pretend that you have $5 to spend. Circle the items that you would buy.

Name _____

Dev Shops at a Yard Sale

Dev wants to buy something special at a yard sale.
Read the word problem. Write or circle your answer.

1. Dev counts the money he has.
How much money does he have?

$ _____

2. Dev wants to buy this skateboard.

How much more money does
he need to buy it?

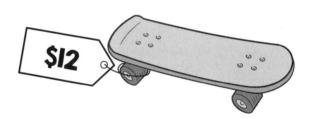

$ _____

3. Dev just got $5 for helping his dad this week.
Does he have enough money to buy the skateboard now?

yes   **no**

Show how you know.

Financial Literacy Lessons and Activities • EMC 3121 • © Evan-Moor Corporation

Name _____

Shopping for a Bargain

Bella and her dad went to a yard sale. Read the word problem. Write your answer.

1. Bella bought three toys. Look at the toys. Use the clues to help you figure out what each one costs.

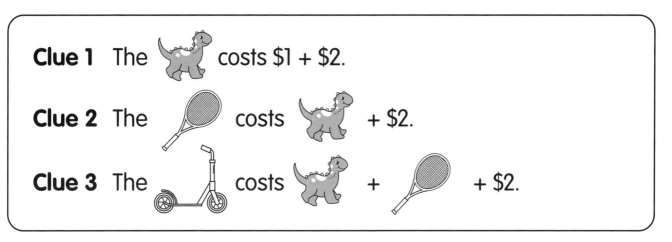

$_____$ $_____$ $_____$

2. How much did Bella spend in all at the yard sale?

$_____$

3. Bella had $20 to spend. How much money does she have left?

$_____$

Come to My Yard Sale

Tell the class that they will create their own yard sale tables and go shopping for bargains.

WHAT YOU NEED

- Yard Sale Items Cutouts, page 111
- My Yard Sale, page 112
- My Bargains, page 113
- play money ($20 per student)

- crayons
- scissors
- glue or tape
- a pencil

WHAT YOU DO

1. Give each student a copy of Yard Sale Items Cutouts and My Yard Sale.

2. Have students cut out five items that they would like to include in their yard sale. Tell students to color their items. Then glue or tape these in the boxes on their My Yard Sale page.

3. Then have students think of two of their own items to include in the yard sale. Have them draw and label each item on the My Yard Sale page and write a price for each.

4. Give each student a copy of My Bargains.

5. Put students in pairs. Have them trade their My Yard Sale pages and "go shopping," choosing what to buy. Remind them that they can't spend more than the $20 they have. When they decide what to buy, have them complete the My Bargains page.

Yard Sale Items Cutouts

Color and cut out five items that you want to sell at your yard sale.

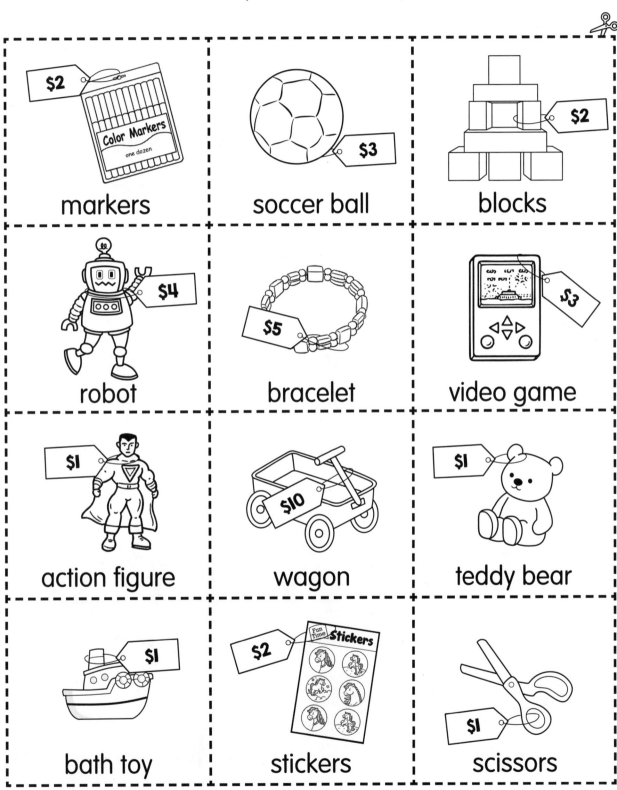

Name _____

My Yard Sale

Write your name on the line.
Glue the five items to sell in the boxes.
Then draw two of your own items that you would like to sell.
Write a price for each one.

_____'s Yard Sale

Name _____

My Bargains

Finish the sentences.

I am shopping at _____'s yard sale.

I have $_____ to spend at the yard sale.

I will buy _____

_____

_____

I am spending $_____ for the things I chose.

Work space

Planning a Party

Understanding the Student Perspective

Young children have probably been to parties for birthdays, holidays, or other celebrations. They are probably familiar with the food, games, and other traditions at a party, but they may not realize that some things need to be bought. Planning a party can help children practice decision-making and prioritizing. It involves making choices about features such as flavor, amount, theme, and cost.

This unit helps students understand the planning and decision-making that goes into a party. A party is a gift we give ourselves or people we care about, and like many gifts, it costs money. The math skills used in this unit include addition, subtraction, and using currency.

Pacing/Lesson Plan

1. Distribute a copy of Surprise Party! on pages 116 and 117 to each student. Read the story aloud to the class as students follow along. Note that the bold words in the story are defined on page 118.

2. Use the Discussion Questions on page 115 to lead a discussion with the class after reading Surprise Party!

3. Distribute a copy of the Words to Know on page 118 to each student. Introduce the vocabulary words, rephrasing or explaining as needed. Then read the directions for the vocabulary practice and have students complete the activity.

4. Distribute a copy of What's the Plan? on page 119 to each student. Read each item to students and provide support as they complete the activity.

5. Distribute a copy of Family Celebrations on page 120 to each student. Make play-money bills or other counters available for students. Read each item to students and provide support as they complete the activity.

6. Distribute a copy of Puppet Party on page 121 to each student. Make play-money bills or other counters available for students. Read each item to students and provide support as they complete the activity.

7. Have students do the Decorate a Cake activity on page 122. To prepare, make copies of Cake Choices on page 123, My Cake Plan on page 124, and My Cake on page 125 for each student. Gather the other needed materials.

 **Discussion Questions**

Use these questions to lead a discussion with the class after reading the story. You may also wish to add your own questions.

- What was Sarah planning? *[She was planning a surprise party for her friend Ajay.]*

- Could Sarah spend as much money as she wanted? *[No, she had $20.]*
  What did Sarah buy for the party? *[She bought decorations, food, and a present.]*

- Have you ever had a party? If so, what was it for?
  Did you help plan the party? If so, what did you plan? What did you buy?

- If you were planning your own birthday party, what kind of decorations and food would you buy?

 Materials

For word problems on pages 120 and 121:
- play-money bills (see pages 10 and 11)
- counters (optional)

For Decorate a Cake on pages 122–125—each student needs:
- Cake Choices, page 123
- My Cake Plan, page 124
- My Cake, page 125
- $10 in play money
- crayons
- a pencil
- scissors
- glue
- craft materials (e.g., glitter, yarn, stickers, construction paper)

 Vocabulary Words

amount	choose	plan
price	spend	

Surprise Party!

Ajay's birthday is tomorrow. Sarah is planning a surprise party for him. The party will be at his home. Ajay will go to his swimming class. Sarah will decorate then! Today, Sarah will **plan** the party. Then Grandpa helps her shop.

First, she goes to a store to **choose** stuff for the party. She has $20 to **spend** on the whole party. Ajay really likes the color red. She gets red party hats, red napkins, and red balloons. She checks the **price** on each item. Each thing costs $2. This is great!

"Your total is $6," says the cashier. Sarah hands over the money. She thinks, "What do I need next?"

"Let's go to the grocery store," she says to her grandpa.

Grandpa drives her to the grocery store. Sarah buys food for the party. The **amount** she has left to spend is $14. She wants to get a cake, lemonade, and ice cream. "Your total is $9," says the cashier.

Financial Literacy Lessons and Activities • EMC 3121 • © Evan-Moor Corporation

"Perfect! I still have $5 left. I need one more thing!" says Sarah.

"What's that?" asks Grandpa.

"I need to buy Ajay a present!" says Sarah.

Sarah and Grandpa go to the toy store. Sarah walks up and down each row of toys. She wants to get Ajay something that he will really like. She knows that he loves animals.

Then she sees the perfect present sitting on the shelf. It is a cute elephant. Sarah smiles, but then she looks sad.

"What's wrong?" says Grandpa.

"This elephant is $6. I have only $5," says Sarah.

Grandpa reaches in his pocket and gives Sarah $1. "Thanks, Grandpa! I know Ajay will love his present!"

The next day, Sarah and all of Ajay's friends hide inside his home. They hear the door open. Ajay comes in. They jump up and yell, "SURPRISE!"

Ajay likes everything about the party that Sarah planned.

"Thank you, Sarah! You planned a great party!" says Ajay.

Name _____

Words to Know

plan	to decide what to do
choose	to make a choice
spend	to use money to buy something
price	how much something costs
amount	how much there is of something

Read the word. Then write it in the sentence. Read the sentence.

plan   Lee likes to _____ parties.

choose   I always _____ chocolate cake.

spend   You can _____ money for
a game.

price   The _____ for pony rides
is too high!

amount   We need a small _____ of milk.

Name _____

What's the Plan?

Read. Circle and draw to do the items.

1. Pretend that you are planning a party. You have $20.
Circle what you would use it for.

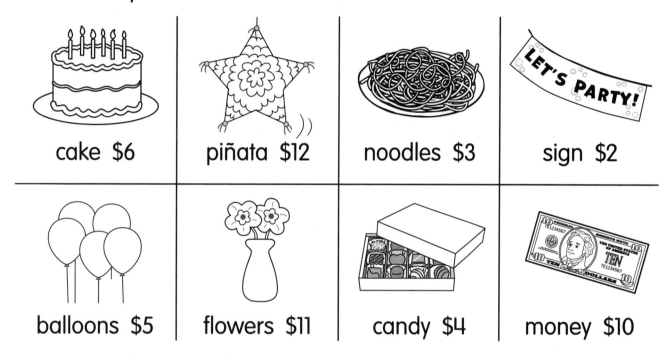

cake $6	piñata $12	noodles $3	sign $2
balloons $5	flowers $11	candy $4	money $10

2. Draw your choices in the party room.

Name _____

Family Celebrations

Read each word problem about buying for a party. Write your answers.

1. Yan has a new baby sister! He lives in China. His family has a party when the baby is 30 days old. They buy new clothes for the baby. They give food gifts to friends who come to the party. Some gifts are ginger and eggs.

This is what they spent:

baby clothes	$12
ginger	$8
eggs	$4

Total: $_____

2. Sofia and her family live in Spain. They have a party the night before the New Year. Each person eats 12 grapes at midnight. They eat cake with good-luck charms baked in it. They also buy red underwear for luck.

This is what they spent:

grapes	$4
New Year's cake	$9
red underwear	$20

Total: $_____

Financial Literacy Lessons and Activities • EMC 3121 • © Evan-Moor Corporation

Name _____

Puppet Party

Marcel, Joey, and Tiki are putting on a party. Read each word problem.
Write your answers.

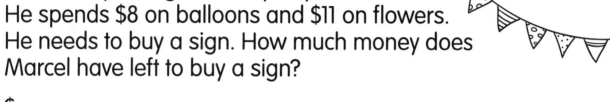

1. Marcel buys things for the party. He has $23.
   He spends $8 on balloons and $11 on flowers.
   He needs to buy a sign. How much money does
   Marcel have left to buy a sign?

   $ _____

2. Joey buys things for the table. He has $10. He spends
   $3 on plates and $5 on cups. He needs to buy napkins.
   How much money does Joey have left to buy napkins?

   $ _____

3. At the party, children will make sock puppets. Tiki buys
   things to make them. She has $20. She spends $10 on socks
   for the puppets' bodies. She spends $4 on buttons for eyes.
   She will buy yarn for hair. How much money does Tiki have
   left to buy yarn?

   $ _____

Decorate a Cake

Tell the class that each student will decorate a cake. They will have $10 to spend. They can choose the type of cake and decorations.

WHAT YOU NEED

- Cake Choices, page 123
- My Cake Plan, page 124
- My Cake, page 125
- play money ($10 per student)
- crayons

- pencils
- scissors
- glue
- any kind of craft materials you have available in your classroom (e.g., glitter, yarn, stickers, construction paper)

WHAT YOU DO

1. Have students think of a party they would like to have. It can be for a birthday, a holiday, or any other special celebration. Tell them to think of the kind of cake they would want for the party.

2. Distribute $10 in play money and a copy of Cake Choices to each student. Tell students to create a cake using the choices shown. They can spend the money you gave them. They can choose one flavor, one icing, and one or two toppings.

3. Distribute a copy of My Cake Plan to each student. Have them complete the page.

4. Distribute a copy of My Cake to each student. Have students decorate their cake according to their plan. They can use crayons and any craft materials available.

5. Have students share their finished cakes with the class.

BONUS

If your students' cakes reflect a variety of cultural celebrations, invite students to tell the class about their celebration: what or who is being celebrated, what kinds of food are eaten, what special decorations are used, and what other traditions happen.

Planning a Party

Name _____

Cake Choices

Choose someone to make a cake for. Circle one flavor, one icing, and one or two toppings for your cake.

Flavor	Icing	Toppings
vanilla cake $1	red $1	sprinkles $1
chocolate cake $2	green $2	nuts $3
carrot cake $3	blue $3	fruit $4
rainbow cake $5	pink $4	chocolate chips $5

Name _____

My Cake Plan

Use your Cake Choices page to fill in the blanks. Then answer the questions.

1. What flavor is your cake? _____

2. What color is your cake? _____

3. What toppings are on your cake?

_____

_____

4. What is your cake for? _____

   Financial Literacy Lessons and Activities • EMC 3121 • © Evan-Moor Corporation

Name _____

My Cake

Use your Cake Plan to make a picture of your cake.

Paying at the Post Office

Understanding the Student Perspective

The post office provides valuable services that let us communicate with others around the world. We use it to send gifts, receive goods bought online, handle bills and other important papers, and even communicate with friends and family. Much communication happens online these days, which students will likely be aware of. But long lines at post offices remind us that they are still important in our communities, and students may not know much about this resource.

The post office provides services for which a lot of effort is hidden from view. We pay for these services a little differently from items in a store, using stamps or paying postage by weight or speed of delivery. The sender pays, even though the recipient receives the benefit.

This unit helps students understand how the postage we pay is used. It sheds light on the many unseen parts of a global service. The math skills used in this unit include one-to-one correspondence, skip counting, addition, subtraction, and using currency.

Pacing/Lesson Plan

1. Distribute a copy of The Mighty Stamp on pages 128 and 129 to each student. Read the story aloud to the class as students follow along. Note that the bold words in the story are defined on page 130.

2. Use the Discussion Questions on page 127 to lead a discussion with the class after reading The Mighty Stamp.

3. Distribute a copy of the Words to Know on page 130 to each student. Introduce the vocabulary words, rephrasing or explaining as needed. Then read the directions for the vocabulary practice and have students complete the activity.

4. Distribute a copy of Using the Mail Service on page 131 to each student. Read each item to students and provide support as they complete the activity.

5. Distribute a copy of Sam's Stamps on page 132 to each student. Make play-money coins or other counters available to students. Read each item to students and provide support as they complete the activity.

6. Distribute a copy of Linda the Letter Carrier on page 133 to each student. Make play-money bills or other counters available to students. Read the story and each item to students and provide support as they complete the activity.

7. Have students do the Envelope Work of Art activity on page 134. To prepare, make copies of one of the Envelope Templates on pages 135 and 136 and the Address Template on page 137 for each student. Gather the other needed materials.

Discussion Questions

Use these questions to lead a discussion with the class after reading the story. You may also wish to add your own questions.

- Have you ever gone to the post office? If so, what did you do there?

- Have you seen someone bring mail to your home? Have you gotten packages? What kind?

- What do people need to do to mail a letter? *[buy a stamp and put it on the letter]*
  Why do they have to do that? *[That's how you pay the post office to send it.]*

- Packages are bigger than letters. They take up more space and are heavier. Do you think it should cost more to mail a package than a letter? Why or why not?

 Materials

For word problems on pages 132 and 133:
- play-money coins and bills (see pages 10 and 11)
- counters (optional)

For Envelope Work of Art on pages 134–137—each student needs:
- a plain envelope
- Envelope Template, page 135 or 136
- Address Template, page 137
- crayons or markers
- a pencil
- scissors
- tape or glue

 Vocabulary Words

mailbox	package	service
sort	stamp	

The Mighty Stamp

Raffi's mom picked him up after school. Mom said, "I need to stop at the post office to buy something."

"What can you buy there?" Raffi asked. "Do they sell posts?"

Mom smiled. "No, the post office sends mail all around the world. Giving people their mail is a **service**."

"But our mail comes to our home," Raffi said. "We do not have to buy anything to get mail."

Mom turned into the parking lot behind a mail truck. "We may not need things to get mail, but we need people. We pay them to move the mail."

"Do you put money in the **mailbox** for the lady who brings our mail?" Raffi asked.

Mom said, "No, we pay for **stamps**. We put a stamp on every letter." A worker was taking letters out of the big blue mailbox.

Paying at the Post Office

Mom and Raffi went into the post office and got in line. There were two workers helping people. Another worker had **packages**. Another put some letters into a machine. There were a lot of people in line in front of Raffi and Mom. "All these people are sending out letters," said Mom.

Raffi's eyes got big. "Look at all that mail!" he said. "Do all these people take mail to people's homes?"

"No, Raffi. There are many, many jobs at the post office," Mom said. "Some people **sort** the mail. Some people drive the mail. Some people fly mail in planes to faraway places. The money we spend on stamps pays these workers."

"Wow! A stamp does a lot!" Raffi said, as they took their turn to buy some stamps.

Name _____

Words to Know

service	an activity that helps people
mailbox	a box used to hold mail
stamp	a sticker that shows that you paid money
package	an item sent in a box
sort	to put things that are alike in groups

Read the word. Then write it in the sentence. Read the sentence.

service We have good wifi _____.

mailbox There are two letters in the _____.

stamp Put a _____ on the letter.

package Look at the big _____ we got!

sort Let's _____ these cookies.

Financial Literacy Lessons and Activities • EMC 3121 • © Evan-Moor Corporation

Name _____

Using the Mail Service

Read. Write and draw to do the items.

1. Pretend that you want to send something to your friend. What would you send?

```


```

2. You will need a stamp. Who will buy the stamp?

```


```

Name _____

Sam's Stamps

Sam is buying stamps. Read each word problem. Write or draw your answers.

1. Sam is mailing a postcard. It costs 40 cents.
Circle the coins to make 40 cents.

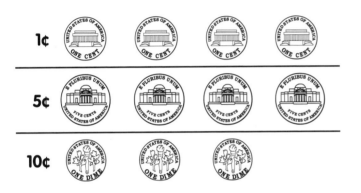

---

2. Sam pays for a stamp using all these coins. How much does the stamp cost?

_____ ¢

3. Sam buys a sheet of stamps. How many stamps are there? Skip count by 2s to find out.

_____ stamps

 Financial Literacy Lessons and Activities • EMC 3121 • © Evan-Moor Corporation

Name _____

Linda the Letter Carrier

Read about Linda's job. Then read each word problem. Write your answers.

Linda is a letter carrier. She goes to the same streets every day. She brings mail to every home. She also picks up mail from every home. All the letters have a stamp. The money paid for the stamps helps pay Linda for her work.

1. Linda picked up 18 letters from people's homes. Each letter has 1 stamp. How many stamps did the people use in all?

_____ stamps

2. Linda earns $20 when she brings mail to 12 streets. She has gone to 7 streets so far. How many more streets does she need to bring mail to?

_____ streets

3. Linda left a package at one house. It had 4 stamps on it. Skip count to find how much it cost to mail the package.

$_____

Envelope Work of Art

Tell the class that they will decorate an envelope to send a special message to someone.

WHAT YOU NEED

- standard-sized envelopes (either card or letter size)
- Envelope Templates, page 135 or 136
- Address Template, page 137
- crayons or markers
- a pencil
- scissors
- tape or glue

WHAT YOU DO

1. Prepare examples: Address a plain envelope and put a stamp on it. Decorate an envelope template.

2. Explain to students that letters and cards are mailed in an envelope. Show them your plain example. Point out the address of the recipient and the return address, along with the stamp.

3. Tell students that they will be writing to someone special and will decorate the envelope. Show them your decorated example. Have them decide on the person they will write to.

4. Distribute an Envelope Template to each student. Point out that they should not draw anything in the three rectangles because they will be covered up later with addresses and the stamp.

5. Have students decorate their envelope templates.

6. Distribute an Address Template page to each student. Have students use a pencil to write the name of the person they are writing to next to "To." Have them write their full name next to "From." Give them another copy if their handwriting is not clear enough.

7. Have students cut out the decorated template and the address templates. Help students attach them to the front of their envelope.

8. Have students write a letter or make a card to put inside the envelope.

9. Students can bring their work home and ask parents to write the addresses, attach a stamp, seal the envelope, and put it in the mail.

Paying at the Post Office

Envelope Template for #10 Envelope

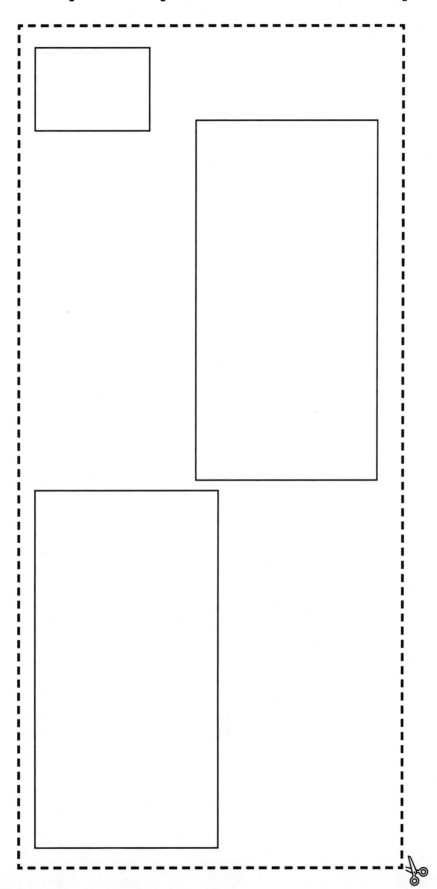

© Evan-Moor Corporation • EMC 3121 • Financial Literacy Lessons and Activities

Envelope Template for Card Envelope

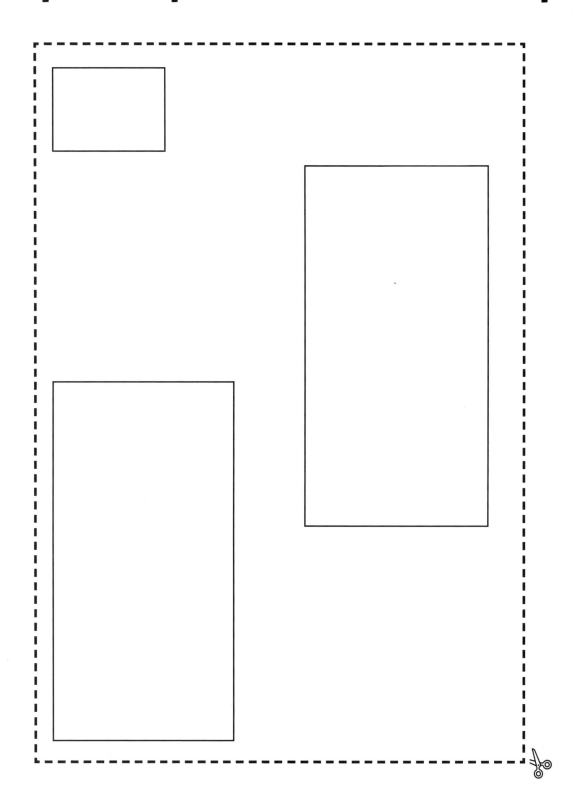

Financial Literacy Lessons and Activities • EMC 3121 • © Evan-Moor Corporation

Address Template

To: _____

_____

_____

From: _____

_____

_____

Answer Key

Using Money to Trade

Page 24

1. coins totaling $1.20
   example:

    1¢

    5¢

    10¢ / 25¢

2. 80¢
3. coins totaling 75¢

Page 25

1. $6
2. $12
3. drawing of 3 buckets

Buying Groceries

Page 36

1. $9
2. no
3. one dollar bill

Page 37

1. $33
2. yes
   Work may vary.
   Example: $33 + $6 = $39. She has $40.

Shopping for Clothes

Page 48

1. $5
2. purse, hat
3. two $10 bills

Page 49

1. Totals will vary, but should match the circled items and add up to no more than $45.
2. both

Earning Money in Your Family

Page 60

1. Answers will vary, but should be worth at least $5.
2. drum, bear, ball

Page 61

1. $33
2. Answers will vary, but each should add up to $12. Combinations can include coins and bills.

Saving Money

1. $7
2. $12
3. $19
4. $11

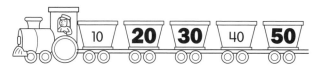

1. 4 times; 2 times
2. $7

Paying at a Restaurant

1. $14 in bills and/or coins
2. Foods will vary, but their total cost should equal $14.

1. $23
2. $4 in bills and/or coins

Raising Money to Help Others

1. $16
2. $30

1. $6 in $1s, $25 in $5s, $30 in $10s, $20 in $20s
2. $43 and 77¢ OR $43.77

Buying and Selling at a Yard Sale

1. $8
2. $4
3. yes; Answers will vary, but should mention or show that he needs $12 and now has $13.

1. $3; $5; $10
2. $18
3. $2

Planning a Party

1. $24

2. $33

1. $4

2. $2

3. $6

Paying at the Post Office

1. coins totaling 40¢
   example:

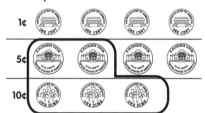

2. 66¢

3. 12

1. 18

2. 5

3. $8

FREE Activities

to Help Children Learn!

Get **free printable lessons and activities** to use with your students or children.

Scan Me!

FREE Samplers

https://www.evan-moor.com/free-samplers

STEAM

Project-Based Learning

Real-World Learning for Tomorrow's Leaders!

STEAM is an approach to project-based learning that uses **Science, Technology, Engineering, the Arts, and Mathematics** to engage children in empathizing, thinking critically, collaborating, and coming up with solutions to solve real-world problems.

Each robust unit in this classroom resource focuses on a hands-on STEAM project that encourages students to enjoy the journey of creating and sharing his or her solutions to help create a better world.

128 reproducible pages.
Correlated to current standards.

Grade 3

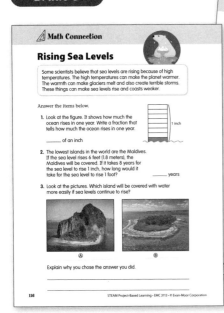

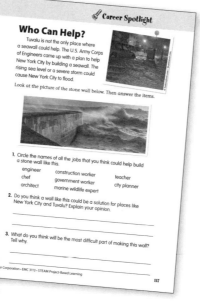

Teacher's Edition*	
Grade 1	EMC 3111
Grade 2	EMC 3112
Grade 3	EMC 3113
Grade 4	EMC 3114
Grade 5	EMC 3115
Grade 6	EMC 3116

Available in print and e-book

Weekly

Grades 1–6

Real-World Writing

Real-World Learning for Tomorrow's Leaders!

Help students explore real-world purposes for writing with activities that demonstrate thoughtful and effective writing strategies.

The **24 writing units** within *Weekly Real-World Writing* focus on six common writing purposes: **self-expression, information, evaluation, inquiry, analysis, and persuasion.**

Weekly activities include letters, journal entries, product opinions, advertisements, directions, interviews, and more!

Units are designed to fit into a weekly lesson plan and include:

- Teacher overview page
- A writing sample to model each skill
- Graphic Organizer for student notes
- Two writing tasks with response pages
- An extension activity

128 reproducible pages.
Correlated to current standards.

Teacher's Resource Book*

Grades 1–2	EMC 6077
Grades 3–4	EMC 6078
Grades 5–6	EMC 6079

Available in print and e-book

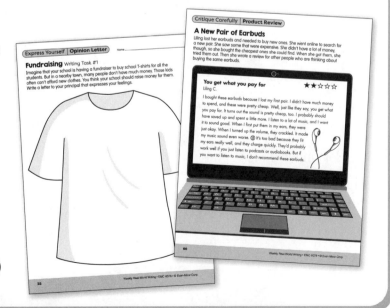

Grade 3

Social and Emotional Learning Activities

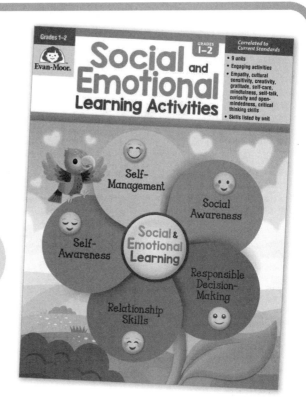

Real-World Scenarios Give Students Important Life Skills!

Support students by helping them develop, identify, and practice positive behaviors and thoughts with social and emotional learning activities. Research shows that SEL experiences improve student achievement, reduce stress, and increase positive behaviors such as kindness, gratitude, and empathy.

Social and Emotional Learning Activities includes:

- **100+ engaging activities** that weave social and emotional learning activities into the busy school day

- SEL instruction that incorporates **writing, reading, math, social studies,** and **cultural diversity**

- **Creative writing, puzzles, games, art projects,** and **real-world scenarios** that engage children in practicing positive behaviors and boost self-image

The nine units cover the five domains of social and emotional learning:

- Self-Awareness
- Self-Management
- Social Awareness
- Responsible Decision-Making
- Relationship Skills

112 reproducible pages. Correlated to current standards.

Teacher Resource Book*

Grades PreK–K	EMC 6095
Grades 1–2	EMC 6096
Grades 3–4	EMC 6097
Grades 5–6	EMC 6098

Available in print and e-book

Grades 3–4

Grades 1–2